Conscious Motherhood

FINDING YOURSELF
in the
BEAUTIFUL MADNESS

CATHY SPOONER

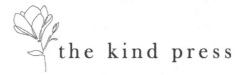

the kind press

First published by the kind press, 2021
Copyright © 2021 Cathy Spooner

This publication contains the opinions and ideas of its author. It is intended to provide
helpful and informative material on the subjects addressed in the publication. While the
publisher and author have used their best efforts in preparing this book, the material in
this book is of the nature of general comment only. It is sold with the understanding that
the author and publisher are not engaged in rendering advice or any other kind of personal
professional service in the book. In the event that you use any of the information in this
book for yourself, the author and the publisher assume no responsibility for your actions.

Cover: Mila Book Covers
Internal design: Nicola Matthews, Nikki Jane Design
Edited by Georgia Jordan

Cataloguing-in-Publication
entry is available from the
National Library Australia.

NATIONAL
LIBRARY
OF AUSTRALIA

ISBN 978-0-6450887-7-9
ISBN 978-0-6450887-8-6 (ebook)

To my darling children.
My love for you brought me to my knees.
That same love raised me back up
higher than I thought possible.
Thank you for being my greatest adventure.
Loving you always, Mummy.

Contents

Preface

I'm standing on the front steps late at night. The kids are asleep, but only just. It's been one of those days, weeks, heck, I don't even know when I didn't feel like this.

I'm numb. Numb from exhaustion, numb from thinking, numb from worrying. I'm numb to life. I feel like I want out, but my life is good so why do I feel this way? I should be happy, but I'm terrified I don't know how to be anymore.

I stare up at the dark sky, searching for answers. Lightning flashes in the distance behind clouds but there is not a sound. *Is that me?* I wonder. *Am I the silent storm?*

My heart feels so heavy the weight makes me want to fall to my knees. I can't do it anymore. I'm so sick of trying so hard all day every day just to feel normal, to feel some kind of something, anything that resembles me.

Where is that girl I was? Have I lost her? Has she gone forever?

I look into the night and feel the breeze cool the warm tears on my cheeks. I whisper the words *I have nothing left*, like they are the only ones I know.

Surrender. In this moment I am completely empty, utterly void of feeling. There is no disappointment in me, no judgement, no fear. Just nothingness.

But it is in this silence that I am able to hear her within me. The truest part of myself, the spirited girl I knew, not the broken woman I have become. She whispers that I will survive this, she still has fight left in her.

In this moment of complete and ultimate surrender, something in me shifts. My miracle happens. My soul speaks up, declaring *I deserve more than this. My family deserves more than this, and things* **will be better.**

Introduction

Welcome, Beautiful! I'm so glad you're here, and by the way, I think you're amazing.

By picking up this book you have made a conscious decision to help yourself. Whether you hunted it down of your own accord, heard about it from a friend or was gifted it by a loved one, I believe it is in your hands for a reason.

There are words on these pages that you need to hear and experiences your soul is craving to have. This book could be a gentle nudge in your back or a whisper in your ear that says just what you need to hear (even if you don't know it yet).

My belief is that reading this now is exactly where you need to be. Breathe that in for a moment. **This is exactly where you need to be.**

One of the most amazing experiences we will ever have in our lives is the first moment when we hold our precious new baby in our arms. The months of growing pains, the hours of labour pains, the stress and the drama all float away in the instant you catch your first glimpse of your baby. Here at last is your new lifelong friend, the unknown soul you've been imagining for months.

This first encounter brings a love you never believed possible. In that very moment, your world is changed forever.

Change brings many variations when it comes into your life. With motherhood you are introduced to the polarities that will forever co-exist. You're surrounded by elation, shock, bewilderment, joy, isolation, community, anger and love.

Over time many of us mothers start to drown in the pressures and expectations of motherhood. Our desire to be the best mother we can be is a responsibility that can become heavy. Out of love we place everyone before ourselves and slowly drift away and lose touch with our inner self. We adopt practices of self-judgement, self-questioning and an unintentional letting go of the courageous woman inside.

Why is it that we lose touch with ourselves and the lives we once held so dear when we become parents? Simply because the majesty of being a mum is like nothing else.

We dive into the world of being a mum with so much love and enthusiasm that we can tend to forget about ourselves and our own needs. We may lose touch with the things in life that make us happy and see friends less often. Our relationships with our partners transform and might lose connection.

These changes all feed into a shift in our perception of ourselves. Slowly but surely, as we stop doing the things that make our hearts sing, as we sacrifice too much and start replacing self-love with self-judgement and self-attack, we unknowingly break ourselves down and pull ourselves further away from grace.

This book was born from the desire within me to understand motherhood better. I spent years searching within myself, at times with desperation, the answer to why I found being a mother so difficult at times. Why I had feelings racing through my mind that no mother should ever feel. Why I felt so disconnected and unhappy even though I had a blessed and beautiful life. Why I just wanted to escape all of it.

Thankfully I came to realise it isn't me that is broken. In fact, I've never been more whole in my life after the journey motherhood has taken me on. What's broken is the story of motherhood we have been following.

The true story of motherhood got lost somewhere as it was being passed down. Real life and its pressures changed our perspective and made us think we needed to meet a set of criteria to "succeed" at this.

Mothers are not broken; our environment is broken. Sadly, it's not the story that is crumbling, it is us mothers.

For too long we have struggled through the years that should have been some of our best all because we feared being judged more than we feared losing out on life. But I'm here to tell you, your story can and will be different. There is a way to embrace all the beautiful madness of motherhood, to find balance and reconnect with yourself again. It's part feeling so terrified of things never changing and part feeling terrified things will change. But if anything, it's taking the leap regardless.

I see you for all the silenced pain, the unheard cries, the longing to be more and for the guilt. I see you. You are worthy of living far greater than these moments and I want you to understand that these moments do not define you, but they will create you new if you let them.

This is your moment, Mama, to let go of all that has been holding you back and live a deeply connected life led by grace.

My Story

My amazing husband, Spooner (whose real name is Tim, but it just feels weird calling him that), our three children, Jacob, Harry and Ruby, and I have a very blessed and happy life.

We were happy. Yet despite all the things I could be grateful for, my life as I knew it changed after the birth of my second son. A world I hardly knew existed had now become my reality as I fell into a dark place literally without warning.

I was diagnosed with postnatal depression, post-traumatic stress disorder and anxiety. That diagnosis felt like it had changed me forever, no one was more surprised and terrified than I was. I was about to learn the hard way that mental illness does not discriminate.

I had always felt like I was a happy person. I always had the ability to stay positive and got great satisfaction from helping people. I looked for the good in everyone and saw the world for all its beauty and not its flaws. I always walked on the path of kindness, was sociable and loved experiencing life and all it offered.

This is not to say that I didn't have my imperfections. I trusted others too much and myself not enough. I cared way too much about what everyone thought of me. I had soul crushing self-esteem issues and never believed in myself. I would over think and worry. I would always say yes when I really wanted to say no. Never once did I entertain the idea that depression would suddenly take over my life.

Deep down, I could feel that something was not right. I was so disconnected from who I knew Cathy to be and no matter how desperately I tried to claw back what little part of her I could hold onto, I only seemed to get further away.

I didn't know what to do with those feelings early on. I had just had my second baby; he was beautiful and healthy and we had the world at our feet. I convinced myself it was the baby blues and so did every other well-intentioned midwife and doctor.

But this was different from anything else I had felt before.

But there was no way I had depression, I believed it couldn't happen to me. I kept telling myself I would feel better once I got more sleep, once my hormones calmed down, once my living situation changed, once my baby settled. I was clinging to these excuses, refusing to acknowledge or believe that something really was up. I just couldn't face that reality.

Plus, I was the mother of a toddler and a newborn, what choice did I have? I just had to keep on keeping on.

I kept keeping on for years after my diagnosis. At times I felt better, and life was good, then another life event would derail me. Over a period of three years both Jacob and Harry were diagnosed with autism and other disabilities and my mum passed away. It felt like I could never get myself back on track. To make it harder, there was always the feeling of my mental health looming over my shoulder.

Was this really the life I was destined for? Was motherhood really meant to feel this way? It didn't take long for me to start to question my own theories on motherhood and all the preconceived ideas about how this "should" all look. I saw the cracks in the story I bought into and perhaps more telling were the cracks I could now see within myself.

The parts of myself that felt most painful and vulnerable were now the spaces where light was flooding in and I was slowly, but surely, healing myself.

I lived through some of my darkest hours in life. But as you will read, I turned my adversity into my strength. There wasn't anything magical about it, or perhaps there was. That magic that resides within all of us, the truest part of ourselves that has the courage, resilience and determination to find more love in our lives no matter what.

I started to listen to my own inner wisdom. I focused on all the joy and love I already had and when those dark times arose, I accepted them and moved forward. Deep within I knew I had to peel back all the layers and get to the core of myself to find my answers on how to live a balanced, wholehearted, deeply fulfilled life as a mother and a woman.

The words on these pages are written from my heart to yours. I have decided to share my journey with you so that you know *you are not alone.*

Whether you're the mother working on your mental health, the mother who feels like she has lost touch with herself since becoming a parent or the mother desperate to make changes and find balance, I hope the words in this book and the journey I'm offering you is one that will change you forever.

On every page, I have given you all of me. Honest, raw, gut-wrenching and real.

We can't truly heal ourselves and each other if we hide behind a facade of lies. Lies and conforming to gain acceptance can feel comfortable and we like to stay in the cosiness of that. But I truly believe that pain lasts longer and is much deeper when we don't look within and try to heal ourselves.

This book was never intended to turn out as it did, but it has been the most cathartic process, offering me deep self-reflection.

These words started with me journaling in an attempt at self-therapy and evolved into something much bigger than I felt I could contain. All the work I was putting in and the self-reflection and soul searching I was doing revealed so much about me that I realised the outcome of this journey was going to be life changing.

When that change came, I felt compelled – in fact, obligated – to share with you what I learnt about myself and how I learnt it.

I hope you will see yourself in some of my stories. I hope these stories become our stories, the new edition of what the journey into motherhood and beyond is genuinely like. I want you to go on that same journey to rediscover yourself, learn to re-love yourself and have the most fulfilling life you can as a mama.

I think it has been one of my longest and most challenging lessons to understand that this process can, and ultimately will, make me stronger. It will make me a better version of myself and a better mother too. I will be able to see myself with the same love and admiration as those around me do. I will also be a better partner who appreciates her own needs and knows how much that contributes to a happy relationship. I will be able to move through the clouds and cherish those special moments with my beautiful children, and I will be able to show my children what it is to be strong.

Please read through these pages and take from them what you need. Some of it will resonate deeply and some will not be a part of your journey. And both are okay.

This is by no means a step-by-step guide to living your best life or curing depression and anxiety. Nor is it going to tell you how to become the "perfect" mama. I'm far from an expert and I know for sure there is no fail-safe way to cross the waters of motherhood. We are each on our own journey, I am simply sharing mine.

This is the greatest of journeys. Our most wild, humbling and rewarding adventure. May this book simply be a companion along the way.

Thank you for inviting *Conscious Motherhood* into your life.

Conscious Motherhood

Your task is not to seek for love, but merely to seek and find all the
barriers within yourself that you have built against it, and embrace them.
— RUMI

Is there ever a day or week that goes by when you don't judge yourself
for making a wrong decision? When you don't feel guilt or shame over
how you feel inside? Or when you worry if you are doing this right?

We feel alone, misunderstood, unsupported, judged and under
pressure. We don't know how to support ourselves lovingly, let alone
ask for the same from someone else.

But what if there was a way to invite acceptance, compassion,
understanding and love into your life? Conscious motherhood calls us in
to accept all of the beautiful madness that is around and within us, and
embrace it all with loving arms.

When we take a conscious perspective on motherhood it is all
welcoming with no judgement. We see that every experience is a lesson.
We understand that there is no right or wrong way to be a mother. As a
conscious mother we witness ourselves in all our divine, messy glory and
let all of that be. We witness with no judgement or shame. We witness
with love and acceptance.

Conscious motherhood, to me, reflects my ability to stay connected
within myself, to be accepting and honouring of myself. Conscious
motherhood does not imply perfection, it is finding peace despite the
imperfections. It is feeling connected to yourself despite the beautiful

madness of motherhood surrounding you.

Because that's exactly what motherhood is – beautiful in one breath, madness in the next. We can't change every aspect of motherhood for the simple fact that raising human beings to their fullest potential is the greatest and wildest adventure we will all undertake, as both mothers and our families.

When you judge yourself do you ever pause to think that creating and raising a human being is kind of a big deal? Like, the biggest of deals. We can be so hard on ourselves for our perceived failures and shortcomings as mothers we often forget what we really are accomplishing in our everyday lives.

Our pain and stress in life arise from resistance; yet those hard edges are softened when we look with a conscious perspective. Being a woman and a mother with this approach softens all our self-judgement, shame and resentment and gives us the opportunity to see from a different light.

So, what does Conscious Motherhood look like in our day-to-day lives?

- Witnessing all of your emotions and accepting them as they are
- Being kind to yourself
- Forgiving yourself even when you don't feel worthy
- Accepting that some days motherhood will feel hard and uncomfortable
- A willingness to lean into and learn from your challenges
- Setting clear boundaries and asking for what you need from yourself and others
- Seeing yourself in others and embracing our likeness and

differences

- Living in this moment now without any concern for the past or future
- Ignoring all the "shoulds" and living life your way

Conscious motherhood is not changing how we do things, it's actually seeing the truth in what we do. It is understanding that when we place restrictive beliefs and structures around motherhood and that journey, we set ourselves up for failure. We become too hard on ourselves and too hard on others. We judge when we should accept. We turn away when we should lean in. We stay silent when we long to be heard.

When we can witness the truth in motherhood we can start to change the narrative that keeps so many women trapped in a box. This truth will help us see that the journey of motherhood is not the same for us all, it is not a one size fits all scenario and that the story of us we have believed for so long does not serve us.

Women try with all their might to do this right. We strive and try to perfect everything within us and our lives. We love with every fibre of our being and then wonder how when we are trying so hard to do it so right... inside we feel so wrong. It's no wonder many of us mamas are stressed out of our minds, feeling overloaded and lost amongst it all. We lose ourselves, our dreams and all reasoning when we don't embrace motherhood with a conscious and loving perspective.

Finding opportunities to welcome conscious awareness through all of this beautiful madness is a process, a new perspective, a new way of living. I want to help you discover what this process looks like for you. That is something we are going to discover together.

This book offers you the chance to delve into your soul's desires and acknowledge what you already know deep down. Whatever you encounter in these pages, please have no hesitation in believing that the words written on them can help you find the truth of who you are.

This is your journey, your exploration and your moment to reclaim and re-love your life.

Inviting grace

Imagine for a moment feeling calm, leaving all your worries behind you and simply letting go. What does it feel like to let go of the past, let go of expectations and fear, let go of everything that holds you back? Letting go of everything and anyone that no longer serves your highest good. Breathe that feeling into your cells. The weight is lifted off you, feel how light you are once you let go. Feel how calm and at ease you are when you're not stuck in the past or future.

This place is where grace resides. It's the pause in between moments. It's the very end of your exhale. From this deeply connected space, magic happens.

This is how it feels when you invite grace into your life. It's about stepping forward with an open heart and welcoming in possibility.

I want to start us off on the path towards grace with an affirmation that we will revisit throughout the book. This affirmation sets your intention for living with grace.

I release all that no longer serves me.
I accept what is.
I invite grace into my life now.

Grace potentially seems like the most unattainable goal you could give to a mother. The notion of finding this silent and present space with no worries feels like the furthest point from a mother's life. Rightfully so – the daily tasks and stresses in our lives aren't screaming peace and inner connection. So how do we find grace when it's the one thing that we need most?

Grace is acceptance, surrender, love and joy. Grace is when you are able to find more of those moments to pause, if only for a split second, to recentre and connect within.

Inviting grace into your life will look different for each of us, yet the process is the same. It's about creating that pause where grace resides in your everyday life, intentionally carving out awareness in your own mind of how you can be more accepting, have more faith and know how to let go.

Using this book

Before we start, I'd like to give you a bit of guidance on how to get the most from this book. It is in three parts, each of which is designed to help you discover different aspects of yourself and your life as a mother.

Through shining the gentlest of lights on ourselves we will begin with the important process of self-discovery. You will be invited to consider the ways you have changed since becoming a mama and acknowledge some aspects of motherhood that may have taken you away from your true self.

Next, we'll look at how you can start to reconnect with yourself and others. This includes learning to accept, appreciate and love who you are now.

Finally, we will learn techniques to consolidate all the great work you have done and explore ways to make sure you are approaching motherhood from a conscious and loving lens.

The chapters within each part have been set out so you can gradually detangle yourself from the patterns you have become accustomed to and learn to break free of your chains. For this reason, I recommend that you start at the beginning and enjoy working your way through, but do feel free to go back later and revisit sections if you wish to do so.

Throughout the book I have included affirmations in support of the issues we touch on in each chapter.

I love affirmations. When I sit and really read them and let them sink into every cell of my being, I find that they alone can be enough to shift my perception.

If you're new to affirmations or are unsure of how they can help you, my advice is don't gloss over them. When you encounter them in these pages, just pause and take in a few quiet breaths, then really feel into the words as you read them. You can earmark the ones that really resonate with you and come back to them again and again. Better still, you can make reminder alerts of them on your phone or put some on sticky notes around the house so they can be a constant reminder to you of the wonderful work you are doing.

Each chapter also includes reflective exercises, mostly in the form of journaling, but I don't want you to go freaking out over that. This isn't homework. It is, however, the process that was at the core of helping me resolve the issues that were feeding my depression, anxiety and toxic views on motherhood. Without journaling, I never would have uncovered some of the messy stuff that was lurking within me, all the things I had done so well at hiding and accepting for such a long time.

I encourage you to get yourself a journal and use it freely alongside this book. At times I will prompt you for your reflections, while at other times you may spontaneously feel the need to get some of your thoughts out of your head and down on paper. No one has to see what you write, and there certainly aren't any right or wrong responses, but it's amazing how cleansing this can be. In much the same way that talking to people helps us feel like a weight has been lifted, writing can help clear all that emotional clutter and baggage we are holding onto.

I understand that journaling isn't everyone's cup of tea and this certainly isn't a 'Dear Diary' type scenario. Even so, I would encourage you to give it a try, as it can be an incredibly valuable tool for you on your journey of rediscovery.

Do bear in mind that your explorations may occasionally be challenging, so please be gentle with yourself as you engage in this work.

Take your time, be loving and kind and remember you are not alone.

Ultimately, this book will represent something different for each of you. What you need in your life right now will be different from what the next mother who reads this may need. I have written this book with the intention that mothers of all ages and stages can embrace and benefit from another mother sharing her experiences. It is for all the mothers who have a deep longing to find themselves again, to be empowered by their own wisdom and live a truly happy life with their family.

This is book is for every one of us, who deserves to thrive.

Part I

Discovery

Our story

I'm on the tail end of what can only be described as a month from hell, no exaggeration here. I feel as though my very limits have been restructured and my self-belief has been rattled deep in its foundations. We kicked off these nightmarish few weeks with both Harry and Jacob falling ill with salmonella poisoning, an 11-month-old and a 2.5-year-old with that kind of sickness is intense and unrelenting. In the middle of this, my body decides it's going to shut up shop and I have two shoulder dislocations in as many weeks. Spooner has been working away from home and was staying away a couple nights of the week. I am stretched to my limits and then when I think I can't take any more, I am stretched further. I've dug deep, although it was not because I want to. No, every cell in my body wants to switch off and tap out. It is all way too hard, too exhausting, too worrying and too stressful, but I dig deep because I have to. There is resentment here. I'm not sure where it comes from, the exhaustion and giving, the feeling like nothing is working out for me right now. I'm a firm believer in signs and lessons...

but what is this? Sobbing tears from exhaustion and desperation.
I yelled at the kids and whinged about my momentarily crappy
existence to anyone who would listen. I am suffering. As the dust
settles slowly, where am I now? I'm still here, this much is for sure.
The feelings that have ravaged me have been so visceral I can't
really escape my existence or the realisation of how much the world
can feel like it falls in on you. But I am stronger. I got through this.
Perhaps not with much grace. But I suppose that is okay I guess
resilience and strength look messy and have rough edges just like
this. I don't know if I believe that strength can be tied up in a neat
bow.

This is the beginning of your journey, Mama. Everything changes from
this point on. When we show up in our lives with a longing for things
to be better and a willingness to make change then miracles really can
happen. All you need to do for yourself is to show up with an open heart
and be honest with yourself. What made you pick up this book and want
to read it?

From here on in I promise to show you the un-filtered version of what
my motherhood experience looks like. At times it may feel confronting,
but I don't need to shower you with all the joy motherhood brings,
you know all the beautiful stuff. I'm giving you me, bare, terrified that
you may judge me but knowing that that thought alone is the holiest of
reasons for me to share my experience in the hope it may help you.

I want to show you there is no such a thing as a perfect mother and
that despite what you think, you're already good enough just as you are.
I want to help you see that the reality of motherhood is far more complex
than the socially accepted version we have been told to abide by.

Before we delve into all my musings on motherhood, I want to use this space as a checkpoint for you to understand where you are at in this moment. Grab your journal and take your time with these… remember, this is just for you, don't hold back, set the truth free on the page, Mama.

---

1. **What are you feeling now, that you wish you weren't?**

   This could be… *sad, exhausted, depressed, depleted, resentful, angry, full of rage, frustrated, uninspired, let down, alone, unmotivated, deprived, unappreciated, weak, tired of trying, disconnected from life, hating my body, envious, anxious, worried, fearful.*

2. **How do you want to feel?**

   This could be… *inspired, proud, successful, happy, calm, balanced, relaxed, committed, stronger, carefree, sexy, grateful, my best self, joyous, powerful, present, carefree, beautiful, intelligent, respected, appreciated, honoured, supported, excited for the future, adventurous.*

3. **What do you want to achieve?**

   Write down one short-term goal, such as *I will achieve my goal of exercising twice a week* or *I will find more time in my week just for me.* Now write down a dream you have. This could be something like *I want to travel with my family* or *I want to start my own business.* Include all the dreamy details.

4. **If there was one thing that would make you happy, what would it be?**

This could be... *more self-belief, more support from my partner, financial stability, a better job, a holiday, a babysitter, a cleaner, more time for myself, starting a new hobby, meeting new friends.*

Read back over your answers and let them resonate within you. This is your starting point. I want you to honour all of the words you have written.

Often mothers are silenced, even by ourselves. We can hear those stirrings of what our soul yearns for but the expectations of motherhood become too loud.

Is there anything on this list you are most drawn to or that triggers some emotion within you? Tune into it. Listen to your body and see what else arises or if you can sense those emotions somewhere in your body.

What do you intuitively feel? Positive or negative, there is no right or wrong here. All feelings are valid.

I'm asking you to do this because when we connect feelings into our experiences, perceptions and goals, they become more tangible. We now have an emotion that is either going to move you away from something or towards it.

Feeling into this journaling exercise will create a new pathway that leads to healing. That's what this is all about. Healing ourselves and healing our children.

Getting real and going within

It's time to get real, to peel back the layers and let our souls guide us towards what we need to discover and lead us to the places where we want to be.

As I've already indicated, your honesty with yourself is imperative to make this process of self-discovery work for you in the ways it should. Remember that your thoughts and feelings are yours and yours alone. No one can dictate them and no one can judge them.

Unpacking the truthful feelings that are intertwined in motherhood can feel uncomfortable but I want you to know you can do this. You want to. The calling within you to make change is stronger than confronting all that is holding you back. These feelings will talk louder until you witness them and heal them.

You're not alone on this one. Every mother has or will have experiences just like yours. It may manifest in different ways but ultimately we are all hoping to shed the heaviness that holds us back and seeking to reconnect with ourselves.

Being a parent is a world of such extremes. It's a world that most of us can't even imagine until we find ourselves well and truly in it. Often it can drive us right to our limits and sometimes far beyond them. But it also gives us the chance to understand more about who we are, what we believe and what we can achieve. That's if we are brave enough to go within and explore the depths of our spirit.

The path of self-discovery is not always easy. That's why you need to nurture yourself along the way – just like you do with your kids. When things come up that are tough, you need to support yourself fully, with no judgement or shame.

I know that on my own journey I have learnt so much about myself. I'm equally inspired by my strength, passion and wisdom as I am by the rawness that resides within me. I'm learning to embrace all aspects of myself, there is no clause on self-love and acceptance. We really have no choice but to take all of ourselves just as we are.

At different stages throughout this book as you remain open to the process you may find yourself facing some unwelcome stuff. It's probably going to feel a bit like that as we wade through the density of the shadow aspect of ourselves.

If something nasty or difficult does arise for you, please know that you are in a safe place. Make no mistake, you are not just reading these words to fill in time. You are here for a reason and this book is designed to gently crack you open and shine a bright light into all the spaces you tried to hold in the dark, and slowly fill that space up with new love and understanding. Be open to whatever happens along the way and turn to your journal as often as you need.

For those of you new to journaling, just a reminder again not to be too concerned about this part of the process. There is no right or wrong way to do it, so just give it a go and don't skip the exercises. Moving those thoughts and feelings out onto paper can have a profound effect on your healing and your recognition of what needs to be healed.

The journey to grace will undoubtedly be a beautiful one, but often we must weather the storm before can see the beauty of a rainbow. Hold yourself in the space of knowing that no thought, memory or unpleasant feeling is wrong.

The feelings and memories that surface on your journey do so for one reason only and that is not to put you through any more pain, angst or judgement; they surface so you can work on them and release them so they are no longer an issue. They want to be freed. Usually, the more significant and important they are for us to work through, the more uncomfortable we will find the process, and therefore the more resistant we can become.

You will most likely find that this work of peeling back the layers, exposing your fears, getting downright truthful and opening yourself to possibilities will bring up some resistance. It's expected, and I'd say essential. It is a natural instinct for us to resist and push back when fear seeps to the surface, but turning away from our shadows doesn't make them go away. We believe there is more fear in facing the shadows but that right there is the bravest act of all.

Understanding resistance

Resistance is thought transformed into feeling.
Change the thought that creates the resistance, and there is no more
resistance.
— ROBERT CONKLIN

Resistance is our protective mechanism. It's the thoughts, actions and beliefs that arise when we feel we could be in emotional danger. If there is a risk we could be hurt, disappointed, heartbroken or fail we will find the tools we need to avoid all of those things. It's the fear of stepping into something new, it's the excuses and reasoning. It is what is keeping us stuck.

But resistance isn't nearly as dense as we believe it to be, it has more of a slime-like consistency. It is stretchy and flexible and when you face the resistance and lean into it, you access a part of your spirit that has been quietly waiting (or sometimes not so quietly in my experience).

Life isn't perfect and it is the imperfect and difficult moments we learn the most from. It is in such moments that resistance surfaces and we are faced with doing more digging and more delving, submerging ourselves in what needs a touch up inside us and examining what parts of us need attention and what parts we can give light to.

Sometimes we don't realise we are learning until the lesson, shift or change within is done.

When resistance arises, know that it has come in all its fierce glory to be your guiding light. It's helping you bring more to the surface so you can shed the weight from your heart and soul and thereby lighten your step.

The sooner we are able to open to the idea that resistance can equal love, the sooner we can truly embrace the benefits it offers us. That's why I encourage you not to bury your head in guilt and disappointment. Don't trick yourself into believing that you are making a mistake, are at fault in any way or have let yourself and others down. That's not it at all.

Instead, you are about to crack open more, learn more, and see more light in your life than ever before, if you are just willing to embrace the resistance. Don't let it be the wall in front of you that stops you from moving forward. Find a way to climb over it, go around it, even go under it, but make it work for you.

It's worth it, I assure you.

Resistance can manifest in all kinds of ways. It is the ways in which life disguises its lessons and hides away your potential underneath these difficult experiences.

Resistance can look like:

- Hitting an emotional wall
- Feelings of sadness and hopelessness about your ability to move forward
- Recurring physical illnesses
- Feeling like the same challenges in your life happen repeatedly
- Reliving the same relationship over and over with different partners
- Compromising your personal boundaries to please others
- Letting go of dreams by dumping them in the "too hard" or "can't happen" basket

- Growing apart from or facing the breakdown of long-lasting relationships and friendships
- Recurrent issues with your children's behaviour
- Making excuses for everything in life that isn't working and not taking responsibility for any of it
- Feeling undeserving of happiness and the good things in your life
- Self-sabotaging when new opportunities arise
- Dismissing your feelings and being dishonest with yourself and others

Resistance is your body's mechanism to keep you shielded from pain and discomfort. Our brains have been engineered so perfectly to keep us safe, but over time what is actually classified as danger has changed. It's not just about protecting our physical health, but our brains will now respond to any threat to our emotional health and feed us information to reinforce all the stories as to why we should avoid this situation.

Remember the last time someone you loved broke your heart? Remember when you tried something new and failed? Remember when you showed people a part of yourself and it wasn't embraced? Let's face it, it's easier to resist and avoid than it is to face up to things, and the path of least resistance is always an effortless default.

But is easier always better? When we choose to avoid "doing the work" we deprive ourselves of an essential opportunity to make some shifts in our lives. Facing the resistance and that internal voice telling us all the reasons we shouldn't take that path takes courage, but on the other side of courage is reward.

The bigger the resistance and the longer you have been holding onto it, the more dramatic, painful, frustrating, confusing and massive your growth will be.

Life will forever be dropping lessons into our laps and that won't ever change. It's not like once we master a lifelong stand-off with resistance we will suddenly be free of challenges. We continue to be given these opportunities to learn, to see the truth, and each time we choose the path of least resistance, we continue to add extra weight to the heavy load we carry with us, and we build up the wall that is blocking our path to the freedom of a light-filled life.

There is so much potential sitting underneath these layers of resistance. As humans, I think we have started being more concerned about living a comfortable life than one that feels fully aligned with what we truly want and who we truly are.

If it feels right for you, take a moment to think and maybe write about the repetitive themes in your life. Are you able to see a pattern somewhere, like an issue or situation you always seem to struggle with? Are there any health issues that are constantly nagging at you? What is it that you always learn the hard way?

Remember to go gently with yourself. As always, no judgement. Just witness and acknowledge where there may be resistance in your life.

After your journaling, read back over your thoughts and then reflect on them using the affirmation below.

I let go of the need to struggle.
I am comfortable with change
I embrace and go with the flow of life.

Hopefully you can see that these patterns are just part of being human and you can begin to embrace that. Learning to recognise and release yourself from certain thoughts and behaviours is an important part of your journey.

As we dive deeper into this process of self-discovery, try not to judge yourself, overanalyse or be too critical. Remember that you are here to find your rainbow, not focus on the storm.

With that said, let's start exploring some of the colours that make up the experience of motherhood.

The mother archetype

I'm not sure if any other moment in my life has come or ever will come close to the magic of giving birth. Those first few moments when I held my precious new bundles of love in my arms are sacred and etched in my memory forever.

That moment when you meet this incredible little soul who has been a part of your very being, connected like nothing else before, it will never be like anything else.

I've shed a thousand tears thinking of my own and other mothers' first moments with their babies. Every one of them is sacred beyond words. Nothing prepared me for the indescribable amount of love I would feel for these amazing little human beings. Without knowing anything about them, I was utterly captivated by their beauty, innocence and purity.

This intensity of love is etched into our beings. As mothers we will protect and love our children no matter what.

Our desire to love our children, over time, feeds a story of what love "should" look like. Love starts to become self-sacrifice. We twist the meaning of love by adding expectation onto an experience that was and always will be unique.

In Jungian psychology they refer to an archetype as a collectively inherited unconscious idea, pattern, thought or image that is universally present. This is what has happened to motherhood. Our understanding of what is expected of us and how this "should" all look is dictated and led by an idea that we have all collectively bought into.

It's safe to say that every mother knows all about guilt, shame, regret, fear, judgement and the pressure to be perfect, but where does this all come from? Part of it starts with ourselves, with that nasty ego voice inside telling us self-limiting stories about who we are and who we should be and why we're failing to be either. What feeds these stories comes not just from our own lifetime and the experiences that have moulded our opinions and perceptions, but is found all around us too.

Without always consciously realising it, we are all subjected to society's pressure about who and what a mother should be, how she should discipline her kids, how much of her life she should sacrifice for her family, what she should wear, what her body should look like and how she should feel.

There is no one-size-fits-all approach to motherhood and trying to tick all the boxes is fragmenting women and the inherent love they have for their children. We believe our love can be measured by whether we are ticking all the boxes or not. Your love is not dependent on all the things you do or don't do. *Your love just is.*

What makes it even harder is that we are not the only ones who absorb these myths about ideal motherhood. Somehow, somewhere along the line it seems like everyone in our lives has become a questioning and opinionated friend, mother or expert. Even complete strangers can't wait to tell us what we're doing wrong and inform us how we should do better, peering judgementally down their noses at us all the while.

As a mother, it can feel like the world around us has suddenly become volatile, restrictive and full of pressure.

Understanding the true essence of the mother archetype shows us just how far away from our own truth we have been led. The mother archetype is a woman who conforms, she fits into a box, she does things a certain, acceptable way. She is doing all the things for all the people. Self-sacrifice is key to her being deemed good or successful. She is driven in the workplace and devoted in the home and this is just what is expected from her.

We aren't understood by society around us and we barely understand each other at times. The differences between mothers seem to create a divide, like there is the right team and the wrong team. Stay-at-home mothers, working mothers, natural mothers, anti-vaxxers, co-sleepers and controlled crying, liberated parenting and strict upbringings.

For the most part I'd like to think that in every mother out there, you will find a unique woman who is living the best way she can in her particular circumstances. Yet many mothers are also doing what they think they "should". They are unconsciously following the mother archetype. The one that says a good mother is measured in how depleted she is, how much she sacrifices herself, how much she keeps on going, how beautiful she looks and how she manages to just do it all.

If you think about it honestly, what defines a good mother to you? How much of those outdated stories about the mother archetype are weaved into your own perspectives and then expectations on yourself?

One thing I have begun to slowly accept is that a good mother is never defined by one moment, one decision or one direction she takes. **She is defined by all her moments.** The challenging and the graceful.

Like so many mothers, I felt a huge amount of disappointment and expectation (mostly from myself) about not breastfeeding my second son, Harry, for longer than we were able. I've always walked the natural path and honoured my body's ability to do magical things. I put both of us through so much in my quest to do what I believed was best for my baby because I had worked it into my head that breastfeeding was the only right option.

My expectation of what one aspect of motherhood should look like unravelled me. When it didn't work for us, I just couldn't accept it. I was left feeling empty and guilty and fell so easily into self-attack.

What I have realised since – and it's taken me years to get here – is that this one decision does not define my "goodness" as a mother.

If we are realistic, not to mention fair with ourselves, we need to acknowledge that we will make many mistakes along the way. More than we will ever want to admit. But this is the reality of raising another human being.

Talk to your own mother figure and I'm sure she will divulge some moments when she felt she made the wrong decision and questioned her mothering qualities. I doubt it is even possible for us to make the "right" decision every time.

There is no manual for parenting and no hard-and-fast rule book either. You don't get handed a list of dos and don'ts the day you walk out of hospital with your new bub. It is more likely that you get told nothing. Any information you do get is often conflicting, confusing and bewildering to say the least.

They tell you the basics about how to keep this tiny human fed and alive, but they don't tell you how doing that will require you to trust your instincts more than anything and be willing to fail and to get up and start all over again.

That's why we are all in the same boat here, fumbling our way through the tumultuous waters of parenting. Sometimes we will make mistakes, while at other times we will get it so right that we surprise even ourselves!

What is important is that these "right" or "wrong" moments do not determine whether you are a great parent or not.

Like I said above, it's the overall impact you have in the lives of your children that really matters. It is the core values you have instilled in them to give them the best chance at a beautiful and happy life. It is the experiences you share with them that will shape their outlook on the world and the way they relate to others. It's the unwavering self-belief and inner knowing you teach them.

It's showing them every day your love does not need to be earned, they are worthy of love just for being.

We need to talk more

Spooner and I pulled up out the front of a tiny shop, the only one on the street, and I had a shy girl moment… did I really have to go in there and ask for a pregnancy test?

Sure enough, the young adults in this community had it tough with condoms, pregnancy tests and thrush medication all hanging behind the counter.

We were on our honeymoon at Kangaroo Island off the coast of South Australia. We had said before the wedding we wouldn't try but we would just stop trying to *not* get pregnant and see what happens. After having an early miscarriage five months before neither of us was pressuring ourselves.

Sure enough, there were two lines. That moment changed me forever. We were going to parents! On the flip side, we also would not be able to eat all the soft cheese and wine that was stashed in our holiday home… nor would our scuba diving adventure and sashimi have been a good idea if we had known!

The images we conjure in our mind about being a mum are often seen through some very rose-coloured glasses. It goes without saying that the beauty of becoming a parent and the joy, rewards and love are more profound than anything. But those first images of our perfect world of parenting don't typically include any of the heavy stuff.

Even when they send you home with this tiny little creation, there isn't much education at all on what it really takes to be a parent. We are expected to know. And when we are hit with a tonne of bricks (because if you haven't been then you're not a parent), we stay silent. We assume that because the gravity of all of this was not conveyed, we must be doing it wrong.

Many of us are still keeping our lips sealed about the sheer madness and struggles that ensue when we bring children into this world. Why are we keeping it all so hush-hush?

The answer is fear. This is what drives us to keep it all in, to not share our struggles and the brutal, somewhat smelly, truth about being a mum. We fear being judged and we fear not being good enough. We fear not being accepted, that our decisions will be criticised, and that our relationships will never be the same again. We fear that by being honest, we are admitting failure or weakness.

Yet if more of us mums were honest with ourselves and others about what really happens and most importantly, how we truly feel about it all, then we would all have fewer issues with facing our fear. Knowing we are not alone and that our fears are not warranted is the liberation that many of us need.

Now, I'm not saying here that all of us sit about keeping close-lipped about the craziness of our lives and bottling it all up. As women we love a good chat and a moment of sharing and we definitely engage in this behaviour often when we all congregate. We can be very forward with our friends or families about the daily challenges we face. But are we being totally honest all the time and saying the stuff we might be afraid to say? Or are we glossing over it all and making it more acceptable for others and more comfortable for ourselves?

I often see women keeping it surface-level, talking about their fatigue and sleepless nights. Focusing on their babies' daily bowels movements and not saying what is screaming inside them. *This doesn't feel right* or *I want out* or *This is so freaking hard.* To speak with this kind of authenticity pulls at every part of our being. No mother wants to feel like she is failing, but you can sure as hell guarantee that when no one is saying what they truly feel, the rest of us will assume we are the bad egg. The rest of us will go further inward and blame ourselves. We will analyse all our faults and let shame take over.

There is no right or wrong. Feelings are feelings. Period. There is no clause. You can feel whatever you are feeling. The good, the bad and the horrendous. It is all just feelings and even though we don't like the negative aspects, everything in life has to have balance. We have to have polarity in everything. If we were never sad, would we truly appreciate what happiness is?

So, if it's so normal, why are we still so silent?

To break the silence we need to get real about the stuff we all want to say but sometimes don't. There are no secrets here. This is about self-discovery, finding the parts of you that hide away so you don't have to face up to the truths you don't like to admit. We can't move forward if we aren't willing to acknowledge the realities of the world we live in and accept that having these feelings doesn't make us any less of a mother, so please leave your mummy guilt at the door.

I am certain we can all relate to some or many (or maybe even all!) of the following statements and feelings about parenthood:

- I didn't expect my life to change quite this much.
- I can't remember what used to light me up.
- Some days I feel so overwhelmed I cry.
- I feel so unappreciated.
- I am drowning.
- Does anyone see or hear me? I feel invisible.
- I miss feeling like my old self.

- I miss sex. God, I miss sex!
- I actually hate sex now, my desire is non-existent.
- I don't even enjoy being around my kids right now.
- I cannot cope with how busy this is.
- I miss working and feeling like a powerful and successful woman.
- I want to stay home and be with my children more.
- I wish I looked after myself better, but I don't know how to find the time.
- Some days the anxiety cripples me and I can't function.
- I have rage in me that scares me at times.
- I'm not sure breastfeeding feels like it's worth it, it's so hard for us.
- I feel ostracised and uncomfortable breastfeeding in public.
- I hate my body.
- I want to eat well and cook healthy food but I'm unmotivated and time-poor.
- I want to exercise but I'm always making excuses.
- I get angry at the smallest of things.
- I feel resentful towards my partner and the freedom they have.
- I feel envious of other mums for their ability to keep everything in balance.
- I constantly feel like I'm not good or worthy enough for the responsibility of motherhood.
- I spend too much time worrying about what other people think of me.
- I'm finding this is just so hard! Is it hard for everyone?
- It feels like my emotions are out of control and my kids bear the brunt of it.

- I feel guilty and overanalyse every parenting decision I make.
- Am I doing enough and giving enough to my children?
- It's easier to eat more chocolate than face up to how I feel about my body.
- I'm desperately needing an escape from all of this.
- I feel like life is escaping me even though I have a blessed life.
- I wish I could have the old me back.

How many of those truths could you relate to? More to the point, how many make you question your worth as a mother? The important thing to remember here is that owning up to thinking any or all of those statements and feelings in no way means you are any less incredible in the role you fulfil each day. It simply makes you human. Your feelings are valid and acceptable no matter what the discomfort level is for you.

We don't often get to see what goes on inside another's mind but all of us mothers will have these feelings at some stage, a common thread that links us, yet we feel scared to speak out loud.

Your mother, sister, friend and mother-in-law, or the soccer mum, canteen mum, playgroup mum and other mums you see around you may be trying so hard to understand why they love being a mother so much, yet still experience these antagonistic feelings. Despite the facade or appearance or your perception of them, what other mamas are going through internally is always going to reflect a similar pattern to you. We are all on the same pilgrimage, attempting to find the balance between the woman we are and the mother we aspire to be.

I know you probably don't believe it now but there can be balance between these two, but for that to occur we need to let go of our old habits and ways of thinking. We have to break down the walls of resistance to create the space for grace to enter our lives.

Let me make it very clear, however, that shifting and changing our thought patterns can be a slow process. Often we have spent years building these concepts up in our mind until we believe them. Realistically then, transforming these patterns won't happen instantly, but there is rarely a quick fix for anything in life, and nor should there be.

Don't be disheartened though. As we will talk about later in this chapter, there are always lessons and love to be found in adversity. It's part of the journey, so know that every step you take towards becoming a happier, more fulfilled and inspired you is a step forward and every one of those baby steps counts.

Much like when our children start walking, we may start out on shaky legs and take some tumbles. We might even cry and scratch our heads in confusion. But ultimately, we will get up and continue to push on, continue to learn and continue to grow.

Life will always throw lemons your way (usually *without* the tequila and ice) and you will constantly revisit these fear-based concepts at different stages in your life. Being honest and sharing your experience with others is really about creating a bigger and brighter future for all us mums. A future in which we don't judge ourselves or each other.

A future, too, where the role of a mother is fully appreciated and respected.

All feelings are valid

There are some days when I feel shattered and broken, tired and exhausted and wholeheartedly over it. I wake up realising my husband has gone to work and it's all on me today.

This has been the structure of our family since the kids were born, but there are some days when I wake up and realise I'm alone and I just don't want to do it. The sound of defeat is a baby crying on the monitor and a toddler in bed with me telling me the sun is up (when for sure it is not). The kids are awake and so my day begins.

In the workplace, these are the days you might call in a sickie, but it's not like that with motherhood. You just get on with it.

For me, these days are often about way more than just being tired. It's because I'm not enjoying my role as a mummy that day or week. The pressures of navigating special needs, therapies, homework, resistance and three-year-old tantrums have left me uninspired. I'm not motivated, I'm not parenting from the best place and I just want a break from it all.

It hurts when I feel like this because the people I don't enjoy spending time with are my darling, gorgeous children whom I love. I struggle to admit to myself without smothering it in a good serving of guilt that despite my love for my children, there will be days when I just don't enjoy my job.

The thing I need to understand – and perhaps you do too – is that my feelings about doing my job of being a mum have nothing to do with my love and devotion towards my gorgeous mini human beings. It's important that you know it is okay to not love your role of being a mama every waking day. You are justified in this.

This is a job with no breaks. It's a job that is so deeply connected to your heart and soul that it calls on every ounce of your strength, love and perseverance. It's a job that you learn and grow from every day, but that growth does not come without a huge dose of hard work. It calls on everything you have and when you feel like you're empty, you somehow find more for them. Then it takes you up to the highest of highs and makes all that stuff worth it.

I've been a stay-at-home mama since a recurrent shoulder dislocation ruled me out of returning to massage therapy. We discussed our options as a family and it made sense for me to stay home with the kids while we were thankfully in a position I could do so.

I have always been grateful for the opportunity to stay home with our kids, I haven't missed a thing in their life and I know I'm blessed to be able to say that. But being a stay-at-home mama meant I could create a clause in there for myself, that because this was my only role – I had to be perfect at it. I had to love it always.

When the reality of that ridiculously high standard hit me, I felt guilt. Instead of seeing the truth here, that motherhood is hard and some days we won't love all of it, I blamed myself for not being a good enough mother. "Good mothers" don't feel that way.

As much as many of us enjoy our jobs and work extremely hard for an employer or ourselves, there is still some level of disconnect there. It's a job, after all. The world won't end if the proverbial hits the fan. But when our children are involved, it is impossible for us to disconnect, and nor would we want to. That connection is deep within our core.

This is why parenting is so demanding. Everything we do with our children from the moment they are born (and even before that) matters. It matters to us as parents because all we could ever want for our children is the absolute best. To let them know that they are loved wholeheartedly and unconditionally every single day. To be there to support them and catch them when they fall. To watch all their achievements in life with incredible pride.

That's a big part of the reason we become parents in the first place. It is to have someone special in our lives who we can help and give happiness to, just as they help and give happiness to us.

Knowing the joy of having children is a beautiful thing, and what we strive for as parents in providing for our children is just as wonderful, but it is tiring and demanding work to create and nourish a human life to its full potential. This is exactly what you are doing. No biggie at all, just creating life, teaching little humans everything about the world, dodging bullets on no sleep. That in itself should tell you that you are already doing enough and you are a great mother.

Sacrifice and selfishness

The mother archetype we spoke about earlier dictates to us what a "good mother" looks like. Part of that story is that we are conditioned to believe that, in order to be the best mother possible, we should sacrifice. This is a concept that all mothers are familiar with. We have to be. There is no possible way you can be a parent without having some form of sacrifice in your life.

The definition of sacrifice is to give up something valued for the sake of other considerations. That pretty much describes being a parent in a nutshell.

It goes without saying that as parents we would give up anything for our children and their happiness, but the issue here is not about what we're prepared to give up. Rather, it's the pressure being put on us to give things up that is the problem.

When we make sacrifices in life is it because we voluntarily agree that it's the best thing to do, or do we do it out of obligation? We aren't given medals for any of this, least not the mother who sacrifices all to the detriment of herself.

Sacrifice seems to start out small, in some ways it's that plant clipping you got from your parent's place and innocently popped in the garden. Before you know it, the vine has tripled in size and is taking over the whole garden.

We make changes in our lives that need to be done when we enter into motherhood, these are the changes that must come to make space for your new family. Then there are the little sacrifices seemingly like not going to the gym, not spending time with friends, saying yes when you really mean no, not resting enough or eating well, or filling your schedule with kids' stuff and having no white space for you.

We can't sacrifice all our needs forever. It just won't work. When we try to, we end up finding ourselves resentful, whether it is towards the kids, our partners, our extended family or work.

Understanding self-sacrifice means we need to understand self-care. It's much more important than massages and getting out for a walk. Self-care is when you prioritise your needs alongside the needs of your family.

Sacrificing yourself will burn you out and leave you angry at life and perhaps those you love most. Trading self-sacrifice for prioritising ourselves is not selfish, it actually makes us *all* happier.

Think of it this way: how much happier are you on those days when you have managed to do something for yourself? Your cup feels fuller, your heart warmer and your eyes more open to the world, all because you did something that nourished *your* soul.

Your children will be happier and more content with a mama who is living in this space more days than not. Let go of the idea that sacrificing yourself will make people happy. It's clear it isn't going to make you happy, so why on earth would your loved ones be happy if you are not?

The only sacrifices you should have to make as a parent are pragmatic ones. It's a given you won't have boozy dance-filled nights anymore (unless you can do kids and hangovers, hats off to you!) and that doing what you want when you want isn't an option. Your work schedule or staying home has also changed and perhaps too your income and therefore, less retail therapy (even though I'm sure we need that now more than ever before). That's a natural kind of sacrifice. But giving up your personal hopes and dreams, your hobbies and the things in life that make you happy cannot keep you happy and nor does sacrifice like that mean you are a stellar parent. What it actually means is that in your efforts to be the perfect mum you are letting yourself down and leaving yourself vulnerable to stress and pressure.

The quest for perfection

The pressure that gets put on us to assume the role of perfect mother is endless. There is so much focus on all the things mums *should* be doing or could be doing to make their children's lives complete and to be the perfect mother.

You need the big house, the expensive school, the nice clothes, perfect kids, the "bounce back in no time" post-baby body, the mountain of extracurricular activities and the immaculate home. You need to look the part and keep it together.

All of this is driven by the warped sense of expectation that society places on mothers. Yet who is dictating this goal post of perfection?

It's the attitude that says you can be it all and have it all. The positive inspirer in me is resisting when I say this, but *I don't think you can be it all and have it all*. All it does is set off a twinge of anxiety inside my gut.

Being it all and having it all in that way requires me to absolutely stretch my limits every single day, not stopping or allowing for errors, and most likely missing out on so many chances to smell the roses along the way. The whole idea just oozes busyness to me, and as a mum, I've had enough of the busy!

Now, I'm not suggesting you should just sit on your hands and not grab life by its horns. Life is jam-packed full of incredible opportunities and we should all be willing to create the life we dream of. My issue is with the focus on being it *all* and having it *all*.

Why would we want to be it all when we are not designed that way? We are each unique and have such differing and individual qualities to offer the world. Why can't we just be happy to be ourselves?

This pressure to have everything and be a super mama is what is breaking some of us apart. Our quest to fit into the mould of a perfect mother is pulling us away from the things that truly bring joy to our lives while we replace them with shoulds, busyness and pressure.

For me, being a "perfect" mum is about being authentic. It means being yourself and being totally unapologetic about it too.

I don't fill our schedule with things and expectation, I may be too soft with my discipline and I'm terrible with time management, but I'm creative with playtime, I love exploring new ways to cook healthful foods and I love being a home body. That's me and I'm owning it.

I'm not going to pretend I'm the mum with a spotless home (even though every time we have guests, I may be wishing I was). I sometimes loathe park play, as I spend most of the time watching one toddler avoid near misses while simultaneously chasing a crawling baby around who wants to eat bark, dead spiders and poop. And I am definitely not the mum who can juggle a multitude of tasks and responsibilities without her head spinning off.

I'm tired of trying to be someone else's version of okay. I just literally cannot do it anymore. Nor should we have to. We should never be trying to fit into a mould, the mould should never have existed.

The more time I take to appreciate and embrace my authentic self, the more I realise there actually isn't any other way. If I don't accept myself as I am then I face the rest of my life feeling stressed, overcompensating, worrying, stretching myself and being disappointed. I just want to be me, and that's more than enough.

It could be argued that our searching and striving for perfection is not entirely a bad thing, as it can encourage us to work harder towards our goals. But how many of us can say we have a healthy relationship with our inner perfectionist?

Perfectionism isn't a trait we can switch off easily, so when we start using it as a tool to reach our goals and motivate us to move forward, we can often find that instead of being the driver behind the goal, it takes over.

Forever chasing after this kind of perfection will only keep us trapped and unhappy because all of us are so incredibly imperfect.

Life was never meant to be perfect and neither are we. It's more about stumbling, crawling and skipping from one moment to the next, so striving for perfection is an endless and unrewarding goal. What happens when you reach it? Can you even reach it and do you want to? Because to embody perfection you may very well have to give away so many parts of yourself just so you can fit into the mould.

True perfection comes from being able to see, forgive and love yourself anyway. It occurs when you can see how incredibly imperfect you are and move forward, minus the self-judgement, by letting go of what you think you should be doing and how you want to be perceived. It's using conscious thinking and perspective towards yourself.

You are your own biggest advocate in this. You must love yourself for all your imperfections, poor choices, mistakes and errors in judgement, not despite them.

Deep down we all just want to be happy. Plain and simple. But our pursuit of that happiness often sends us on a doomed mission for the things we imagine will bring contentment to our lives, cue here a killer body, the latest swanky handbag, a shiny new car, an immaculate household, a well-paying job, kids who are top of the class, kids who are well mannered and behaved all the time, being the superstar mum who juggles everything effortlessly.

This pursuit is driving our need for perfection in the wrong direction, because none of these things will make us truly happy. No external factor can generate genuine happiness within us, yet our ego persists in telling us that she knows the way to happiness and it's through perfection.

If anything, perfection can only bring us heartbreak and disappointment. The goal of being everything to everyone is simply too heavy and crushing.

If only we could see that the real and truest version of ourselves is already everything it needs to be, we could stop trying to compensate for our perceived faults and lack. If only we stopped trying to make everyone else happy and accepted ourselves as we are – because it really can be as simple (and as difficult) as acceptance.

I release all that no longer serves me.
I accept what is.
I invite grace into my life now.

Giving ourselves a reprieve from perfection is one way we can allow more grace into our lives.

In her book *The Gifts of Imperfection*, author and researcher Brené Brown says: 'Perfectionism is a self-destructive and addictive belief system that fuels this primary thought: If I look perfect, and do everything perfectly, I can avoid or minimize the painful feelings of shame, judgment, and blame.'

It's the child within us trying to be perfect and avoid the pain.

Being the truest expression of yourself is the only way, any other way is too painful.

The darkness

_____ Journal entry _____

*I am completely and utterly over it. I feel exhausted and I'm sick of
trying to feel better. I just want to be happy again. I just want to feel
like myself again. It all just seems so hard every day. Today is New
Year's Day and after a few days of feeling horrible I made a promise
to myself that I wouldn't let this depression beat me. I refused to
give in and promised myself I would fight for as long as it took. But
right now, in this moment just hours later, I don't want to fight. It is
a feeling of despair. It all just feels too hard, and I know that sounds
like a total cop-out, but I'm just tired of this consuming my life. I
want to live a normal life again. I don't want to ever feel like this
again, not for a single moment. I want to have enjoyment in my life
again, like I used to. I want to be able to stay calm, like I used to.
I want to be able to see the world how I used to. I don't think it's
too much to ask to be given the chance to have my life back. I don't
want the one I have now. It's hard and it's sad. I feel like my real
life has been stolen from me. Getting depression wasn't something
I did to myself. How or why I was picked to face this journey is*

something I don't understand. But sitting here now thinking about how long it could potentially take me to feel like myself again, well, it terrifies me. I am scared about the life ahead of me.

It's hard to know how we got to that place where mothers being depleted and highly stressed is normal and acceptable. Women are struggling when they should be thriving and it's all "part of the deal". We are crumbling under the stress and expectation and we do so mostly in silence. Women are depressed, anxious and unhappy and trying to give what little they have to those they love.

It's so much bigger than having a nap, it's systemically ingrained in us that we must prioritise everyone before ourselves to fit in with the expected version of motherhood. And that expectation is draining us of all our possibility.

Motherhood is challenging at the best of times, with the polarities in life possibly never more present than when you are a mama. Too many of us are living our lives treading water, perhaps without even realising. Worse still, too many of us are drowning.

You're not alone in all of this. We all have our moments. Sadly, these moments are becoming more frequent. There is more to being a mother. It does not need to be overshadowed by expectation, pressure and judgement.

Motherhood can have balance, we can take care of others without sacrificing ourselves, we can feel fulfilled without guilt. We can have joy and responsibility together; *this is all possible*. But we need to first acknowledge that something here is broken and we need to take action to make lasting change and we need to, because we mothers deserve more than this.

Understanding your stress

I'm not sure I've ever known a mother who doesn't at some point look like a fragile mess. There is no question about it: raising children is a stressful job.

Our darling kids are learning how to develop into adults with all their kinks in perfection just like us. They need to learn boundaries, adopt appropriate behaviours, gain understanding about life and themselves and learn who is their safe space. And of course, on some days they just drive us mad!

The process of growth is challenging for children. While trying to understand all these new feelings and experiences they turn to their safe people because they know no matter how much they drive us up the wall, we will always love them. That unconditional love is beautiful because it fosters a wonderful and safe space for them to explore all of the new life feels with us as a security blanket.

However, if only this knowledge made it easier to manage the stress for us. The smallest and simplest of daily actions with children become complex, tiresome and frustrating. Simple instructions to them need to be repeated several times, with an escalating tone and volume each time. Time must be spent chasing after your son who has managed to stealthily grab a pair of scissors from the kitchen bench and thinks it would be a total cack to run around the house with them. Effort has to go into cleaning up the mess your daughter left on your bedroom carpet after she used the contents of your makeup bag as supplies for her latest craft and painting activity.

These are seemingly funny situations that we may be able to laugh at in hindsight, but at the time they're happening, they can ramp up our stress levels very easily – especially when we are already in an elevated stress state (yes, that's pretty much all mamas on the daily).

So how do we avoid this stress? While we cannot always control our children's behaviour, we can control our reaction to it, which in turn can change our body's stress reaction.

Stress-inducing situations can creep up on us and if we don't see them coming it can be harder for us to stop our reaction. Kind of like once that steam train has momentum it is very hard to slow us down and make wise decisions.

Having an understanding and awareness of what triggers our stress and when we are in a potentially high-stress situation is a lifelong tool all mothers need. All we can do is try, we won't be perfect at it every time, but if we can lower our stress response half of the time, we are already creating new neural pathways and behaviours.

---

1. **Become aware of your key stress activators**
   Try to pay attention and learn what it is that stresses you the most.
   Motherhood is busy, often we can't articulate what our biggest trigger is due to so much going on. Is it the nagging, the mess in the house, not having enough time to yourself, having too many things on your plate, not practicing enough self-care, kids bickering, kids not listening, your partner not supporting you or helping out? I truly could go on for a while here, but you get my point.

2. **Recognise your stress as it begins to creep in**

   Often when we are caught up in the whirlwind of a stressful moment, or several moments running back-to-back, we tend not to notice our stress until it reaches its peak. By then it's usually too late or at least very difficult to reign it back in and control the storm before it totally engulfs us.

   It does take time to train ourselves to start recognising the stress building up from the beginning, but catching it here means we have more chance of changing direction and shifting our thinking into a more positive and constructive light and avoiding our stress reaching its peak.

3. **Witness and release the stress**

   In order to be able to shift our thinking, we need to take the power away from the stress. Much of our stress is fed by fear, and taking power away from the fear is the only way we can truly overcome it.

   Witness the stress. Say to yourself *Stress is only a state of mind and I am able to change my state of mind.*

   Take some deep breaths in and out, and imagine whatever is causing you stress to literally be blown out of your mouth as you exhale. Visualise it as grey or dark mist, feel it in your body when you think of it. The anger at the kids, the tiredness, the frustration at your partner, the self-destructive thoughts – *exhale* them all out. Then breathe in light and positivity. Visualise your breath and body being filled with light. Feel your heart expanding, your body softening.

Repeat this as many times as you need to until you feel calmer. You can do this in the car while the kids scream at the back of your head or locked in the toilet, we mamas are pretty resourceful like that.

It's a powerful moment when we realise we can shape and shift our mood and feelings simply by witnessing and releasing them.

This technique of awareness, recognition and release can be used again and again, and the more you develop your skills in applying it, the stronger the outcome will be.

We won't be able to eliminate the stress we experience as parents but we can help to control our reaction to it, which is probably way more important.

The effects of long-term stress on our emotional wellbeing and physical bodies can be devastating when it's left unaddressed. High levels of cortisol can cause short-term symptoms like headaches, digestive dysfunction, anxiety, depression, weight gain, low libido, insomnia and irregular periods.

For a fast fix, I find breathing is always the answer. Head over to my website to get a free downloadable with different breathing techniques to help calm, balance and reset your nervous system.

Part of releasing the stress is also normalising that these feelings and experiences are normal. It may not feel nice, we may wish to switch it off but stress is part of the deal with motherhood. If we can look at these moments with conscious awareness and know that it just is what it is, then we reframe the stress. We move out of fixing and resistance and into a conscious loving perspective.

Helping yourself feel calmer and more in control is essential for being able to be the best mother for your children. You cannot function at such a high stress level forever, something will give. Remember you may not be in control of your environment, but you do have control over your mindset.

The realities of exhaustion

You can't put into words the type of earth-shattering and soul-crumbling exhaustion that descends upon you when you become a parent. The best of days can quickly become a nightmare and a major struggle once that fatigue sets in.

Some days, I'm not even lucky enough to start off on a good foot because after dealing with a teething baby, a toddler who has nightmares and my own mind racing and running through *all the things*, I wake up looking like something out of a zombie movie. Worse still, I drop the kids at school with my shirt on inside out.

Fatigue and exhaustion force your brain and body to resort to their absolute bare essentials to enable you to keep functioning and surviving.

I'm sure you've all heard about the studies that show how sleep deprivation affects not only working memory but long-term memory, decision making, vigilance, stress adaptation and physical functioning. On a chemical level, sleep loss activates your sympathetic nervous system, which is responsible for your fight-or-flight response (think basic cavewoman instincts). This leads to a rise in blood pressure and heightened levels of stress hormones like cortisol.

Not only that, but sleep loss makes it harder for the brain to communicate between its different sections, meaning that total brain and body function are affected.

Essentially, poor sleep equals mama at fifty per cent capacity, maybe less. Think about those days when you've had a total of four hours of broken sleep with a newborn and you either lose your thought mid-sentence or even stop talking altogether, as if the simplest of words have vanished from your memory.

Gone are the days when you are exhausted and you can just sleep whenever. Now when you are exhausted or fatigued, your body just has to keep on going, while still being subjected to the tiring, constant madness that is making you tired in the first place.

And let's not even mention how brutally tough your world becomes when a new baby arrives and you already have kids to look after!

Before I had my own children, I remember a friend telling me after the birth of her first son that you don't truly know what sleep deprivation and fatigue are until you have children. That statement could not be truer! You know you will be tired and grumpy, but until it actually hits, I don't think most of us can conceive what pressure it can put on our physical and emotional wellbeing. It is a whole new level of tired.

This fatigue surprisingly doesn't get much better as the kids get older. We may not be nursing a baby through the night, but we still have trouble falling asleep and having a restful sleep. We have overactive minds, high stress levels and end up wired and tired. We go beyond the fatigue stage and our bodies flip in the other direction and start buzzing despite being so deeply tired.

When I am tired and run-down, those days are by far my worst. The deep kind of cellular exhaustion that happens to mothers isn't something that is fixed with an afternoon nap (but please, please still get in those naps when you can). We literally feel like we are at our breaking point. And often we are.

When your body and mind have been pushed to such limits, you are functioning on the most animalistic part of your make up as a human being. You're just trying to function, nothing more, so luxuries like patience, compassion and levelheadedness aren't always easily accessible.

Be gentle on yourself.

As much as this issue is much deeper than ducking away for a nap, after three kids, and learning the hard way, here are a few approaches for helping you to feel better now.

Sleep when they sleep

I'm sure you've heard this one from your mother and in-laws, but it is surprisingly difficult to instigate and stick with. I still get annoyed when my hubby tells me to try this, like it's the simplest thing to do, but I know he is right.

If you can manage to ignore the laundry to be folded and messy kitchen for long enough to get your head down on a pillow, you will be eternally grateful. All the sleep gurus say an hour's sleep during the day could be equivalent to several hours at night.

Ask for help

Often as mothers we can fall into the trap of feeling like we gotta do it all on our own. If your mother is over for a visit, ask her to hang out the washing or mind the kids while you head out for a walk. Ask your partner to do dinner that night.

You didn't go into this parenting journey to be the sole carer for your kids, and that mindset is limited and self-destructive. You are good to nobody if you're dead tired from trying to undertake every task on your own.

Be kind to yourself

Everything is worse when you're tired. The days are longer, the whinging louder and the crying more ear-piercing. Even simple things like eating feel like an effort and you really aren't anywhere near your best, so be kind.

If you lose your temper, that's okay. If you forget something important, that's okay too. If you feed the kids stale bread and honey for dinner, yep, it's all okay. Forgive yourself for being human.

Give your body the fuel it needs

One of the problems with being tired is that it can become harder to make healthy choices.

When we are exhausted, our bodies instinctively go for fast, high-energy snacks like chocolates and carb-rich foods, rather than the healthy salad that will give us more nourishment. We can't be perfect with our nutrition every day, but just keep in mind that those calorie-dense foods are a short-term fix and when you're dead-to-the-world tired, your body needs more than that.

Protein will keep you running for longer, and filling your body up with nutrient-dense food will keep your energy at a steadier level.

Some days the only fix is a melted cheese sandwich and an extra-strong coffee, I get it. Just do what you can.

Breaking point

As parents, we have an endless list of stressors that can accumulate and push us to our *breaking point*. An accumulation of stress, fatigue, lack of sleep, and physical and emotional imbalances all compound together and leave us feeling loaded with too much of life. Add into that the daily mini-stressors of children who know exactly how to push all our buttons with such precision (just how exactly do they do that?).

Your cup can only take so much. At some point, if you aren't emptying it out, it will overflow and you will reach your breaking point. Some days this looks like a stress explosion, anger, rage and a need to escape the pressure. Other days it may look like the deepest kind of sadness, sobbing uncontrollably, feeling flat and despondent, and having no motivation to do the next thing.

The one thing that cracks your breaking point may not even seem that bad as an isolated incident or experience but it was just the last bit that overflowed your cup.

Often, as mothers, we then feel awful that this huge outpouring of emotions doesn't exactly correlate to what just happened. We feel guilty towards the kids and then even question if we are losing it. But we are not. We have no space for anything else and our body will reset in whatever way it needs to. Whether that feels nice to us or not.

Sometimes, when the catalysing moment really isn't anything big but provokes such strong emotions, it is coming from someplace else. When we start to realise that these stressful moments are usually fed by a build-up of hidden emotions and root causes, it's easier to accept and surrender to those strong feelings that come up for us. This can enable us to see how and why we got that point, as well as give us clues about how to release the fear that is attached to it.

Throughout our lifetime we create a story about ourselves that is shaped by all of our experiences. It contains both positive and negative chapters. It is filled with our perceptions and interpretations.

When we have perceived an experience as negative, we imprint that moment into our brain. We store it there for later and when another experience arises that triggers those same feelings of, say, unworthiness, self-doubt and insecurity then all the feelings attached to those past experiences that haven't been healed come flooding to the surface.

Our underlying negative beliefs about ourselves are triggered and activated when a stressful situation arises, and instead of being able to see our current situation for what it is, we are pulled deep into that negative story. Truth here doesn't seem to matter as much as our own belief. If we believe we are unworthy and so on, then it is so. And our current experience not only triggers our pain response but it gives us feedback to support the same limiting beliefs.

I am an open book with a big, exposed heart; you can probably see my emotions coming before I am. I express freely and don't have an issue with letting most people see my vulnerable side.

But I haven't always been like that. I was definitely sensitive, emotional and different growing up but over time I lost that (hello the shit storm of living through your twenties and trying to be everything you are not). I told myself that I shouldn't feel a certain way, that certain feelings weren't acceptable and I started bottling stuff up. Mothers do this so very well.

As we talked about earlier in this book, we attach a should or shouldn't to each emotion and determine whether it is okay for us to feel it or not. If not, we stock it away, store it in the catalogue of 'I will not be loved and accepted wholly if anyone sees this within me' or 'Feeling this way makes me unlovable'.

Being loved is our greatest and perhaps our only core requirement as a human. So much of our life here on Earth challenges that very belief that we are worthy of love just as we are.

Children are our greatest teachers of all. My experience since becoming a mother has cracked open and exposed all of those limiting stories. Every single one of them as they surfaced had a physical manifestation of me reaching my breaking point or breakdown.

The big ones, some of which I'm still working through, would send me spinning many times. I would get triggered again and again by the same behaviours from my kids whilst I continued to live and follow the same limiting patterns and not making change.

As parents we often focus so much on what we can teach our children without realising that in fact, by their very existence and just doing what kids do, they present us with the opportunity to see ourselves for all our self-limiting and false stories, for all our mistakes and errors in judgement, and to love ourselves regardless. Perhaps to love ourselves because of all those things.

This is when I realise that women, and mothers in particular, are genuine superheroes. We are holding onto that restrictive and limiting weight from the past whilst helping our children find their feet in this world and carrying the load that is placed on a mother's shoulders. We may struggle through this and it will be some of the hardest years we ever experience, but we do it. We change ourselves. We change our children. We change the future for other mothers. We are much braver than we realise.

But bravery does have a cost for many mothers. This struggle between being a "good" mother and honouring all within ourselves is deeply challenging. It triggers all the things. It makes you question yourself, sometimes attack yourself. For many, it makes you lose hope. Trying to find your balance between all the things that are placed on your shoulders and fulfilling your own heart feels impossible. It's why so many mothers suffer in silence; they struggle when they should be thriving and they breakdown under the pressure. We have too much on our shoulders.

I'm not even sure how we try to shift the way we have created motherhood to be, but I'm determined to try. We have a world of broken mothers who are unfulfilled. We have mothers in the deepest of depression wasting away on the inside. For God's sake, we have women who would rather take their own lives and their children's instead of admitting to anyone else they are drowning. If this doesn't scream to us all that we need change, then I don't know anything else that would.

Where do we start? My heart tells me it's within. If we can turn within ourselves and each tiny piece by tiny piece heal ourselves, then we have a chance.

I'd love to go smashing through all the patriarchal walls that told us we have to be it all, do it all, sacrifice ourselves and be silent whilst we do it (and perhaps there is a time for that). But I know we can rewrite this story by doing what women do best... we love. We love like no one else can. We have compassion and empathy. We are nurturers. We need to start nurturing ourselves and by that I mean all-in, no-judgement, full acceptance of ourselves in all our messy glory. We need to have that unconditional love for ourselves that we so desperately seek from others.

When we all love ourselves with this kind of tenacious abandon, we heal ourselves. We start to realise that these limiting and false narratives we are living our life in accordance with do not serve us.

As we start to heal ourselves, we will have more capacity to heal others, to lead by example, to be way showers for our children and following generations.

I often find myself wondering what the world will look like for our children. I ponder how much things have changed since our grandparents were new parents and how far from that we seem now. Living now grants us so many privileges and gifts but that comes along with expectation. Too much of which is breaking us down.

Perhaps it is about taking it back to basics. Simplifying life. Lessening our stress so we don't keep crumbling and breaking. Speaking our hearts and our biggest fears no matter how scary that feels. Is there any other choice?

The mental illness epidemic

I remember the very first day I had a panic attack like it was yesterday. I remember the endless nights when I would cry myself to sleep. I remember feeling so alone and wishing to be my old self again. I remember feeling so deeply sad for a reason I couldn't explain. I remember being handed a prescription and told I was depressed and it's okay, this is all normal.

Nothing about any of this felt normal. I had never felt a fear like that ever in my life.

I remember the stress and intensity that was raging through my body the day of my first panic attack. I felt like I was so on edge, and for no particular reason, but I couldn't bring myself back down. I was tightening and tightening as the anxiety wound me up. It was physically painful and emotionally it destroyed me.

It was that evening that I realised something within me was not well. It's hard to ignore an experience like that. It was the culmination of years of me trying to do everything right, of feeling deep guilt and failure and thinking that was all normal. It was the beginning of the biggest struggle of my life. It was also the beginning of my homecoming.

It's quite painful for me to look back to those years, especially those early months after Harry's birth. I feel like I was a different woman back then. I look at her like she is separate from me. My heart aches for her and I desperately want to hold her.

"Incredibly hard period of our life" comes nowhere close to describing that time for me and our family. Being told you have a mental illness and handed over a prescription for a drug to "fix" you doesn't actually make you feel any better. A diagnosis just affirms your worst fear – that something is wrong with you. It gives you answers on why you feel the way you do, but the shame is still there.

Why am I failing at being a mother? That wound right there is the deepest. When you begin to question why you are failing at motherhood it will rip everything up from inside you. Growth will do that, but mental illness takes you on a deeper journey within. It won't leave any stone unturned until you are freed from it. It's a journey reserved for some of the most courageous women I know… and it's taken a long time for me to realise I am one of them too.

Understanding mental illness from the outside is hard. It's hard even when you live within those four walls yourself.

When you live with a mental illness you can have moments, and even days or weeks, when you feel completely normal and like your old self. It does not always look like deep sorrow on the bathroom floor or lying in bed for days. It is a deeply internal experience and I believe so much of what we see on the outside is a speck compared to what's below the surface. We only let people see what we want. We make the rules on our own vulnerability and how much we let people into our internal world.

For mothers with mental illness there is deep fear of judgement and shame so opening up and expressing how they feel is the last thing they want to do. If you can hardly admit to yourself that you need help, admitting it to someone else is impossible.

For those of you reading this chapter and finding something striking you deep in the heart, please know that you are stronger than you believe yourself to be.

As impossible as it may feel, *you need to believe in yourself.* You have to keep reminding yourself that you have done this before, you have gotten through the bad days and the terrible days and the days that were even worse than that.

Setbacks do not mean you are failing; they are just part of the process. And don't forget that a setback automatically implies that you are actually moving forward.

Some days you will feel like you don't want to live this life, you may be so blessed and adore your family but your suffering feels too much to bear. Whenever I have these moments, I remind myself of something that always gets me through: *I would never be given anything I cannot handle.*

The courage and resilience that you show up with every day are phenomenal. Mental illness and parenting should never have to be bundled together, the responsibility of caring for another human being in that way when you need to really care for yourself is an incredibly demanding situation.

I know you don't want to handle it, in fact you would give everything up to be able to feel normal again, to not have this looming in the corners of your life every single day. But one day it won't. One day the intensity of these moments will ease, in some cases, it will be gone. *This is not your forever.*

Walking yourself out of this will feel like a desperate journey if you try and do it alone. Please don't try to do it alone. Women need connection and community. You need to be nurtured in a way that you can't do all for yourself; in fact, trying to do all the things to "fix" yourself just places more on your plate.

If there is ever a time in life to surrender your sword and drop to your knees, it is now. Don't be afraid to open Pandora's box, what is within is your weapon. If anything, I beg you to be so open about your feelings that it makes you uncomfortable because if it's uncomfortable coming out of you, imagine what it does to you when you hold all of that in.

There is no shame in doing this, despite what you or anyone else might think. The only way any of us can heal is by allowing ourselves to receive the support we need. We all have to find a way to move beyond the toxic feelings that inhibit not only our personal growth but also our daily functioning. You deserve to feel better than this... and you will.

Shockingly, one in five mothers is diagnosed with postnatal depression or anxiety. In your circle of friends or your mothers' group there will likely be someone who is struggling with their mental health. Even more worrying is that these numbers do not include much data on perinatal depression (during pregnancy), and they don't capture all the women who are not diagnosed and suffer in silence from either the shame or not understanding their symptoms.

It's heartbreaking to hear these numbers. When I was first diagnosed the number was one in eight - more of us are drowning. It's clear the way we are trying to do motherhood isn't working. We need to embrace conscious motherhood like all our existence depends on it – and perhaps it really does.

If you are concerned about your mental wellness but don't know what to do next, the best thing I can advise is to talk to someone you trust who knows you very well. Someone who will hear all you have to say, honour it and really see you.

If you don't feel you have that with a loved one then reach out to a healthcare professional or call a local support provider like PANDA here in Australia, or the equivalent in your country. They are trained, experienced and have huge hearts and are ready to help support you in whatever way you need.

Please remind yourself every day, you are not failing at motherhood. You are a good mother. Right now, your body and mind need support to get you feeling back where you need to be to thrive and flourish.

You don't need to judge yourself here, Beautiful, feeling like this is way more common than we are willing to acknowledge. You are not alone.

Self-judgement

For as long as I can remember I have cared too much about what people think of me. Whether it was the clothes I was wearing or my personality, if someone had an opinion then I cared what it was.

This insecurity was encouraged along by low self-esteem, which then fed my destructive ego and self-judgement.

Since becoming a mother, I have found I am even harder on myself. I expect the absolute best of myself as a mother, wife, friend and person – all the time. I've set the bar so high for myself I've almost made failure imminent.

We judge ourselves partly because we raise our own expectations and because our self-worth is low.

After my diagnosis of postnatal depression and anxiety I wasn't sure if I could tell anyone. Part of me wanted to, like there was a deep desperation to release some of the pressure building within me. But mostly I was terrified. I knew the moments those words came from my mouth I made it real. Once something is real, we need to attach a reason behind it– why did it happen and who caused it? That blame and judgement will always fall on us.

Part of me still truly believes that if I tell people I have postnatal depression, they will instantly think I can't cope as a mum. Mental illness equals failure. That's what I first thought myself when it all came crumbling down around me. I kept asking myself why on earth I could not cope as a mum. It is such a rewarding and beautiful privilege to have children in your life, so why couldn't I deal with it? I wondered if that meant I was not quite as cut out for this job as I thought. All "good mothers" cope, don't they? The fact I couldn't just proved that I was not a good mother, right?

Surely if I came to this conclusion then everyone else would be thinking the same thing. The fear of telling someone outside of myself and Spooner made me feel a disappointment in myself I had never felt before. I felt vulnerable to the point of shame. I also felt scared, the reality of whether I would be deemed a "fit" mother plagued me. Would my own husband and loved ones continue to believe in me forever or would I lose their trust? These feelings around my diagnosis were crippling.

The beautiful reality is that any nice and decent human being who cares for you will not think you are a bad mother. Whether it is mental health issues or all the complex emotions that motherhood has called you into, we will always find space to judge ourselves and question it all, even when others don't hold that same perspective. Most women I work with are saying the same things.

- Motherhood is hard.
- I think I'm failing.
- I'm a terrible mother at times.
- Some of the thoughts in my mind I wouldn't dare tell a soul.

The more I hear others saying that being a mother is so goddamn hard the more strength I get to set aside my self-judgement. Self-judgement can only thrive in its own isolation. When we are all working through the same challenges, having the same unnerving emotions and feelings, then this isn't about individuals anymore, it's about the collective experience of motherhood.

Knowing you are not alone in this is the most empowering moment.

I'm no longer just one individual "messing this up", instead, I am just like every other mama who is doing her best.

I remember searching online for someone who felt the same as I did, looking at forums and using the dreaded Google to help determine what was going on in my head. I needed to hear that it wasn't just me who felt this way. I had to know that my experience was not an isolated one.

I didn't want to know that another mother was struggling (I wouldn't have wished this on anyone) but in my own moments of desperation to survive I started seeking out evidence that there was someone like me. It felt safer knowing that my feelings were not born purely of my own failure as a mother.

I guess it all comes back to setting such high standards for ourselves that we would never expect anyone else to live up to. When we fail or falter at these unrealistic expectations, we start judging ourselves, tearing ourselves apart and further breaking down the strong woman inside us.

The one person in the universe who deserves our love more than anyone else is ourselves, and yet we are usually the one person we deny that love because of our ridiculous and unmanageable expectations.

I want you to take this message to heart: You, just as much as anyone else in the entire universe, deserve your love and affection.

If we don't love ourselves with full acceptance of our own entirety we cannot flourish and blossom into the best version of ourselves.

The way I see it, self-judging and self-criticism is a form of self-harm. We may not be physically hurting ourselves (although for some women this is how their pain manifests), but mentally, it is breaking us down more than we can ever realise.

Judgement is a nasty thing to inflict on anyone. This is what lurks behind racism, sexism, homophobia, religious arguments, school bullying, and the list goes on. It implies that something or someone is wrong and something or someone else is better.

In actual fact, we are all equal, unique and perfect in our own way. Just because two mums conduct their daily lives in different ways does not mean one is right and the other wrong, and it definitely does not mean either should be subjected to judgement by themselves or anyone else.

Any form of judgement, whether to yourself or to others, will only ever act as a barrier to your authenticity and be a gateway for guilt, fear and compliance.

Mum guilt

Guilt is the one thing inherited as you step into motherhood that we all wish we could leave behind. It's born from the space of wanting to give your children and family the very best of yourself. The problem arises when we attach guilt to situations, experiences or behaviours that we deem are "wrong".

As mentioned previously, there really isn't anything wrong with what you're doing as a mother, it's the framework of expectation that is faulty, not you. Conscious motherhood entails that we look at all our experiences, decisions and feelings with a loving awareness and acceptance. When we don't take this approach, we end up in the mum guilt spiral very quickly.

At the very moment I am writing these words, I still feel it. I'm unsure if guilt ever really leaves you. Even when I know better than to judge myself or be hard on myself for a decision, reaction or thought – I still feel guilty.

My experience with guilt would be much like yours. It's always there, we shape our reactions and behaviours around it without even realising. We say no to doing something for ourselves because mothers don't ever put themselves first. We over think and worry about our parenting decisions and convince ourselves it's our fault. We remain stuck in the past on issues like breastfeeding, birthing and routines. We shush our dreams and desires because mothers dream for others now, not themselves.

It's like a deep-seated root that attaches in our hearts and won't let go. It finds a space to bind in our hearts because all of this guilt originates from love, but then somehow the expectation and story of motherhood morphs that love into unhealthy guilt.

For me, the guilt is at times as fresh and raw today as it was when Harry, my second son, and I began our breastfeeding journey. Honestly, the only thing that has healed this wound for me is time.

As I mentioned earlier, my depression was diagnosed after Harry's birth. Little did I know that it would have a much greater impact on me beyond my emotional and psychological state. My body also responded to the stress –anxiety, constant worry, fretting, over thinking and self-analysis – and the result was that I struggled to breastfeed.

Now, I would never have said I am a champion breast feeder, and let's face it, there are few women out there who are. For something we are naturally created to do it definitely does not always come easily. It's a tough job and I believe breastfeeding and the challenges that come with it are not spoken of and supported as much as they should.

I was able to breastfeed my first son, Jacob, successfully to the age of five months, even then that felt like it wasn't long enough. My physical health was struggling after severe blood loss during his birth, which resulted in breast milk supply and quality issues. We persevered but, in the end, ceased breastfeeding much sooner than I originally hoped.

With Harry, however, breastfeeding was a struggle from day one. I had attachment issues, bleeding nipples for weeks on end and repeated mastitis, while he had terrible colic and suspected reflux.

To say it was a stressful time is an understatement. I just assumed that breastfeeding was my right. I wanted to do it and had done so in the past so I figured this time would be no different, but every feed began to be stressful. I started to hate feeding time as all it represented was pain and stress for both me and Harry. I felt guilty that I couldn't provide for him what he needed and do what as a mother I "should" be able to just do.

Instead of being able to enjoy the bond with my gorgeous boy, I was left in a sea of tears, hoping the ordeal would be over soon. I was longing for our connection and for those magical moments in the middle of the dark, rocking on the chair when I would whisper all the I love yous I could. But we never had that. The despair and guilt I experienced in those moments is something only another mother who couldn't breastfeed can know. This was not how I imagined it would be, and I kept asking myself how this could be happening. Worse still, I blamed myself.

Our early days together were overshadowed by questions, stress and sadness. After being advised by our paediatrician to try Harry on formula, I reluctantly gave it a go. That was the first time he slept for more than an hour, yet instead of being elated and thankful, I felt gutted. It destroyed me that my milk was what had been causing my son so much pain and discomfort. I had persisted for what felt like a lifetime, struggling with his feeding, and beating myself up about it every moment of every waking day.

Guilt was driving a wedge between the nurturer in me and the truth. I couldn't give him what I naturally should have been able to… and that tore me up every day.

At the teeny age of six weeks, Harry was no longer being breastfed. The very weekend I reluctantly made that decision was the same one at which I had my first ever panic attack and it was the beginning of my breakdown. The guilt of not being able to breastfeed him and the enormity of that expectation I placed upon myself was the last straw.

I had held so dearly to the concept that I wanted to breastfeed and I should be able to breastfeed that when it didn't happen, it broke me into pieces. I hardly left the house as I was terrified of people judging me when I fed him a bottle in public. I stayed away from mothers' group and shopping centres. Even with family, I felt ashamed and humiliated that I was denying my baby what I thought was best for him. The guilt overtook me and consumed me.

Having trauma around breastfeeding is very common in motherhood, especially so for new mothers. I am all for natural alternatives for everything in life and I do wholeheartedly believe that breast milk is best. But this does actually come with provisions that we never hear about. Breast milk is best when the mother is *nourished* and well, not when a mother is deprived, stressed and exhausted, leaving the quality of her milk like water. Likewise, breast is best when a mother feels she is emotionally and mentally stable and well enough to endure the process confidently.

This happens to women too often and we are left feeling guilty because our own milk wasn't nourishing enough for our bubs. We blame ourselves; we stress more, which in turn again affects the quality of our milk and our mental wellbeing.

The other provision is that breast milk is best if that is what you *choose*. There are many reasons behind why women choose not to breastfeed and we are not here to judge and make it all harder. The 'breast is best' and natural campaigning may be true based on facts, but life is much more real than that. Placing those expectations on women make them feel less than a good mother when they don't do the one thing their body is designed to do.

Preaching of breast is best actually reinforces stress and expectation on mothers, and if they can't or choose not to feed this way it can be soul crushing. What is best for baby and mama has to be assessed on an individual basis, with no judgement.

Equally so this applies to breastfeeding women who are ostracised for feeding in public. This is a whole other ridiculous conditioning from our patriarchal society that views breasts purely as sexual objects, not as life-nurturing assets. Women should never be made to feel guilty for feeding their babies in public, this is a natural thing to do and I'm kind of tired of watching poor mothers awkwardly try to cover up under a myriad of blankets just so everyone *else* is comfortable.

Honestly, just let all of us women feed our babies in the best way we can. Don't judge us for having breasts or a bottle... a woman feeding a child is beautiful. Full stop.

You have nothing to feel guilty for

Guilt can come in many shapes and guises and it can sneak up on us when we least expect it. From the moment our little ones are conceived, it's there and it doesn't go away. We unintentionally twist normal experiences, decisions and feelings to give ourselves a reason to feel guilty. It's fed by the story of the archetype and overtime I believe our egos become addicted to it.

For your ego, the worse you feel about yourself the safer you are from any outside danger and pain.

Let me give you just a small snippet of the different ways that mothers allow guilt to thrive in their lives. Some of these examples may stir up passionate opinions about what is right or wrong, but that's not what this is about. Remember that every individual has a unique experience.

None of us has the right to pass judgement on any fellow human being. That's why I encourage you to read the following list with an open mind and open heart, without any judgement. Just acknowledge within yourself how many of these you can associate with.

I feel guilty for...

- Not feeling one hundred per cent excited about my pregnancy
- Drinking alcohol before realising I was pregnant or during
- Letting myself go during pregnancy
- Not sticking to my birthing plan
- Having medical intervention during labour, whether it be pain

relief, caesarean, et cetera

- Not being able to breastfeed, either by choice or natural occurrence
- Not giving enough time to my other children when my new bub arrived
- Having zero patience and tolerance for my kids
- Being moody, hormonal and snappy towards my partner and kids
- Leaving the house while my young kids scream and beg for me to stay (this is the worst)
- Attempting controlled crying
- Losing my temper at the kids
- Feeling today like I don't want to be Mama anymore
- Losing touch with my girlfriends
- Yelling at my kids, like all the time
- Birthing a beautiful sleeping baby
- Not having sex with my partner as often as I used to or would like to or think I should
- Feeling like I just want to be "selfish" and have time just for me
- Enjoying work
- Desperately wanting to escape it all and get away
- Having a night off for a date with my partner or a catch-up with friends
- Not exercising enough or eating well enough to get back my pre-baby body
- Letting my child watch more television than I like just so I can have a break
- Crying and feeling overwhelmed

- Not spending enough quality time with my kids, reading and doing educational activities
- Not giving my kids all the latest devices everyone else has
- Practising a little self-care by getting a massage or having my nails done
- Leaving the house an untidy mess
- Not doing the things a good housewife and mother does
- Our children's choices and decisions in life (I've let them down)
- Wanting success in something outside of motherhood
- Working long hours in a job I love or hate
- Feeling like I over-discipline or under-discipline my child
- Telling my child no even for a for a genuinely good reason
- Having irrational and horrible thoughts about motherhood
- Wanting more than being "just a mother"
- Saying yes to anything that is purely for myself and no other

Reading that list may feel triggering for you and that's because we will all see ourselves somewhere in it. The more of these examples we can relate to the more we have our life structured around guilt as it dictates all our decisions and emotions. Yet, it is incredible how many of these items aren't any cause for guilt at all.

So many of our beliefs regarding what we feel guilty about are driven by our ego and fuelled by preconceived ideas that we and others put on ourselves about how a good mother "should" feel. They are not driven by truth and reason.

None of them need an explanation either. You could be sleep deprived. You could have reached your absolute limit with a nagging toddler. You may not be enforcing enough you time with corresponding amounts of self-love and care. A decision may have been taken completely out of your hands. A conversation you had may be influencing your self-perception. Or perhaps you are simply making decisions according to the best of your judgement and knowledge.

My own sense of self and lack of internal belief created the perfect breeding ground for guilt. In any situation in motherhood, we need to realise that we are a product of our own environment, but also of our own mind. What you think enough of, you will become. If you associate normal and acceptable thoughts and behaviours in motherhood with failing, then you will always fail.

You cannot change this experience of motherhood into something it is not. Just because it is not spoken about openly does not mean your lived experience is not normal, acceptable and experienced by many. All of what you feel is common.

So, if it is common, we could come to the conclusion that there isn't actually a place for guilt at all. Because if it's happening to many of us, then we aren't failing and guilt no longer exists. I've avoiding saying normal here because although these feelings and experiences are common, I want us to shift out of the mindset that common means normal. I don't want to normalise it because I don't want this to be an acceptable way for us to continue the story of motherhood.

But again, it comes down to what we perceive as normal. As long as this story about motherhood stays the same, we will forever be living in a perpetual cycle of guilt and self-sacrifice. And I know that the beauty and magnificence of motherhood would not be gifted to us if that was to be overshadowed by expectation and guilt

I remember on one of my low days I was driving in the car with Spooner and running through the guilt procession in my head. It was the same every time. I had nailed the process. I would analyse and break down all the feelings I had and all of my actions. Then I would let the whole lot loose to bounce around unrelentingly inside my head. Thinking, worrying, laying blame on myself, thinking some more and never coming to a healthy solution. (This part is where we get stuck… it's addictive ruminating and obsessing on our feelings.) Eventually that weighs down on me and I'm somewhat broken so I go seeking external comfort and reassurance.

Like every time I go down the guilt spiral, I didn't believe in myself enough to acknowledge that the guilt I was feeling was coming from a place of falseness.

On this particular day, I asked Spooner if he thought everyone else was thinking I was a failure and that I was a bad mum. His response was honest, to the point and very wise (as his responses usually are).

He simply said, "You are the only person who doesn't believe in you and honestly, no one else really cares all that much about your life. They are too concerned with their own."

The gift in his statement was that he really put it all back on me. He made me look at how I was feeling and prompted me to get real with myself about the negative story I was running through in my head.

His words reminded me that I had the power to change that story. He reminded me that when I'm in a guilt spiral, I will often go looking for external validation that yes, I am a bad mother. I start worrying about what other people think and that feeds into my guilt.

But I'm not really looking for validation that I am a bad mother, that's what my ego is telling me and, on the surface, it looks and feels that way. Really, I'm looking for my way out of the guilt spiral… I'm looking for someone to see me and say 'You're doing a great job'.

At my most vulnerable I just want to be seen. I don't actually want to rip myself to shreds and spend so much time worrying about everything

I could possibly ponder on; no, I want my heart to heal and feel better.

Guilt feels horrible in every cell of us. It makes us do horrible things to ourselves and denies us the very things that will free us. Yet guilt is the greatest gateway to your own sovereignty.

If you can witness your guilt and accept it as it is, you will witness all the spaces in your heart that need healing. Under every stone of guilt you turn over is a reflection of what you seek or that which needs to be healed.

How do we become brave enough to turn over those rocks and find what's underneath? We already are brave enough; we just don't know it yet.

The only way to move past such emotions and limit how much they entangle themselves in your daily life is to acknowledge that you feel them. Hear what your heart and mind are saying. Recognise what you are feeling and ask yourself why you are feeling that way.

Then, accept the feeling and surrender yourself to it. Be in it and let all the emotion consume you, just for a moment or for as long as you need. Blocking out emotions and numbing ourselves to feelings never ever helps us move forward constructively, so take the time you need to experience what you feel.

Then, once you have acknowledged and accepted your feelings, forgive yourself. See the situation for what it really is and recognise that guilt need have no part of it. Allow yourself to believe you are worthy of forgiveness, and understand that it is okay to feel guilt, judgement and shame. Those feelings make you no less of a human being. If anything, they make you more of one.

When the mum guilt is taking over your life, or any type of guilt for that matter, remember that you control this feeling. This is not an emotion that is unattached to anything special or important. It's an emotion that is driven by fear.

- Is this guilt serving me?
- Is this guilt reflecting back to me something I genuinely did wrong and need to apologise for?
- Is this guilt coming from the fear of not be the perfect mother or not being good enough?

When you shine a light on these stories, they lose their power. You have the choice and power here to witness your guilt then let it go.

The toxicity of resentment and envy

When you're the parent of children with special needs it truly is a life like no other. I well up with tears every time I think about how fortunate we are to have Jacob and Harry in our lives. If you ever need a wake up call on life and what matters, spend time with these kids. They will show you a world you never knew existed.

Alongside this joy comes some great challenges. Challenges that I don't see other mothers having to experience. That reality can feel hard to bear at times, that perhaps things won't ever get better. That perhaps this reality and the struggles we face being a family of additional needs will always be like this.

When you're faced with an uncertain future you can feel intimidated by or envious of anyone around you who isn't in that place. If I could undo all the letters and labels that have been attached to our boys, I don't think I would. Part of that is of course appealing as it would imply, I could take away their struggles, yet then they may not be as magical as they are right now.

Yet there are days when I wish Autism, ADHD and Speech Apraxia were not our reality. I wish we didn't spend all our time at therapy. I wish my thoughts weren't always racing around sensory needs, calming them, what food made them act out or how to get a task completed. Some days I wish I had a "normal" life like every other mother. Some days I feel resentful that this is the journey we must navigate.

It's uncomfortable and confronting for me to say these words here, trying to be the perfect mother takes on a whole new level when your kids have special needs. "Good mothers" don't talk like this.

The reality is, they do.

Good mothers speak their truth, no matter how painful. No matter how much I fear you will judge me for saying that some days I wish my life was simpler like yours. That I'm envious of how easy it seems.

And then I stop... because it isn't easy for any of us. It's just different. Every one of us has challenges that can't be measured.

My envy of wanting what other mothers have doesn't come from me not loving my life or my kids, it comes from depletion. I only ever feel like this when I am spent and looking for ways to make life easier.

Whether we like to admit it or not, we all feel this way from time to time. As we know, becoming a mother means you make sacrifices and when we sacrifice, we sometimes feel like we are missing out. This can lead to us feeling resentful towards the people we want to blame for us missing out, or we may become envious of those who we perceive are not missing out like we are.

These are all very relatable emotions. It's like the grass is greener syndrome. One thing to remember is that we are never wondering about the grass on the other side when we are content and thriving in our own lives. We almost always fall into resentment and envy when we are unbalanced, exhausted and looking for alternatives or ways to fix all of it.

Resentment and envy are fed by your ego. It's your ego that sulks when others get to go on holiday and you don't. It's your ego that envies your husband for the ease of his life as a parent. It's your ego that becomes envious when your neighbour and her kids have all the latest and greatest things yet you struggle to pay the bills. It's your ego that says you're missing out on something.

Your ego is filled with the limiting aspects of yourself, the side of yourself that wants to stay "safe" and play small. It externalises our fears as blame and resentment so that we don't have to address the underlying issues of imbalance or not prioritising our own needs.

The way to move through this resentment and envy is with gratitude. Fear, comparison and self-sacrifice are behind them so being grateful for what we already have can help to quell those feelings.

No matter what is happening around us we all need to practise gratitude in our everyday lives.

I know the world can sometimes seem so imbalanced. There are people living with a seemingly endless supply of material possessions while others struggle to make ends meet or, worse still, are living in poverty. Some people appear to breeze through life without facing any real tragedy while others' lives can be torn apart by loss and other dramatic events.

It can seem so unfair and unjust. The only way is to embrace and be truly grateful for all that you have. No matter how small the good things in our lives may seem, at any given moment we need to feel deep gratitude for the fact that we have them in the first place.

Whether it is writing your blessings in a gratitude journal, reciting them under your breath or saying thank you for each gift in your life, practising gratitude and being consciously aware of your good fortune can help resentment and envy slowly fade into the background of life. When we aren't lacking in our own lives, we stop seeking the grass on the other side.

Being able to feel thankful for those beautiful moments in your life is also about just being in the moment of your life. It's about being present, making the most of the gifts you have, and not wallowing in the past or stressing over the future.

Really, the biggest way to be thankful and to be free of resentment and envy is to actively participate in, enjoy and relish your life as it is right now. There will always be hard times when life is more challenging, the ebb and flow of life will never change, but it is how we approach the good and the "bad".

Can we be grateful for what we have even when we feel it's hard to do so?

Realising your own worthiness

When you get to a place where you understand that love and belonging, your worthiness, is a birthright and not something you have to earn, anything is possible.

— BRENÉ BROWN

The feeling of not being good enough or feeling unworthy is usually at the root of every fear-based emotion and action we have.

If I don't feel good enough to be successful in my career, I'm never going to really strive and give it a go. Why bother when I'll most likely fail anyway? If I don't feel good enough at being a mum, I will tear myself down and feel guilty instead of believing in myself. If I don't feel good enough to be a sexy and lovable woman, I will make poor health choices, make excuses and place blame and resentment on others.

I can remember growing up and always being a hesitant and cautious child. I really wanted to get in there, have a go and have fun, but the nervous child in me spoke louder than the adventurous one.

Our eldest son, Jacob, is exactly the same. I see the hesitation in his eyes when it's time to ride his bike or do something that requires him to believe he can do it, and my heart quivers a little. Such a sensitive little man he is, just like I was as a young girl.

I don't remember exactly when my cautiousness and lack of self-belief turned into a feeling of not being good enough. Somewhere along the line most of us girls face the shift as the world we grow up in starts to dictate what girls and women should do, say, feel, and look like especially about themselves.

For those like me, and perhaps for Jacob one day, our sensitivity and lack of self-belief can very easily be the birthplace of your I am not good enoughs.

We all have some of this within us. Some of us are genuinely more confident and care less about what others think. Some of us are very good at masking it all. Some of us, you could pick our insecurities a mile away.

Sometimes I wonder if I could change just one internal belief about myself –if I truly believed I am good enough – how different my life and my pain experience could have been.

But clearly, that is not my life, nor is it my lesson.

Obviously with age there comes a sense of being more content with ourselves, and in most cases the older we get, the less we seem to give a crap about certain things.

I used to watch in awe as women in their fifties did exactly what they wanted, expressed themselves freely, chased their dreams and loved their bodies. Society has labelled this a "mid-life crisis" but to me, it looks like a shedding of your not good enoughs. It is what it looks and feels like to know you truly are worthy just as you are.

Until then we must learn to unpack some of this, which can feel like really hard work at times. Our self-doubts still seem to be lodged deep within us. They can stem from the feeling of being unsupported as a child, from destructive relationships, from failed and toxic friendships, and most importantly, from us – from our own ego.

I am not good enough. That one sentence is like a poisonous seedling that twists its tendrils into every decision we make. Without knowing – and genuinely believing – that we are good enough and worthy of everything life has to offer, we make it pretty impossible for ourselves to take the leap and create the life we truly want.

The word "enough" doesn't sit right with me because it implies there is a measuring stick we are trying to get to and until we do, we are failing.

You no longer have to try to measure up to some standard of impossible perfection with your good enoughs. Without loading that expectation on ourselves, we can be free to adapt and develop ourselves into our truest version, the one we were always destined to be.

It is your birthright to feel worthy. You have every right to feel good about yourself, to believe in your own value and to take every step in your life in alignment with your truest self.

Ultimately, living in self-doubt and allowing your "not good enoughs" to fester leads you into the life of an imposter, where you are not living your truth nor revelling in your authenticity. Instead, you are merely portraying a false and limited version of yourself.

We are all guilty at some stage of letting everyone see the version of ourselves we feel comfortable with at any given time.

Since becoming a mother my perspective on everything I do has changed. I am now an example to my children, as they watch, mimic and are shaped by the people and the environment around them – especially by their primary caregivers. They are sponges that absorb everything they see and hear.

This means the worthiness I have crafted for myself is on display to the observant little beings in my life. They believe what they see when they are little and take everything as it comes because they are too young to question the deeper meanings in life.

If they are seeing a mummy who doesn't believe in herself, doesn't trust herself, doesn't put much value in her own worth and believes she is not good enough, then this is the story of self-worth I am showing them.

I know I am a big softie and at times a pushover too, but one thing I want my children to know about me is that I'm a believer. I believe that even on my darkest days, I can find the light. I believe that no matter how tough things get, I will always find a solution. I believe that I deserve a life of happiness and having my dreams fulfilled. I believe that with love I can overcome any obstacle.

I want my precious children to see that despite the madness, the tears and the guesswork in my parenting, *I believe in myself.*

Self-belief and worthiness work hand in hand. Belief is what keeps you going, it's the fire in your belly and the determination to take care of yourself no matter what. The result of that strong self-belief is a deep knowing of your own worthiness.

Before we move on from this topic, I want to introduce a really valuable exercise that will help you remember and believe in the many and wonderful ways that you are, quite simply, worthy.

Analysing our level of worthiness is a common thread that runs through all areas of our lives. Whether it be in our parenting, our careers or our relationships, we are constantly using old stories our ego feeds us to determine whether we measure up.

What I've come to realise is that more often than not, my own self-worth scale does not correlate with what others around me see in me or believe about me.

I was so tightly wound in my self-sabotage that I was unwittingly seeking any excuse to make myself feel more unworthy, because that unworthiness gave me a pretext not to show up and give it my best every day.

Those excuses helped convince me why things were so hard sometimes. By holding onto them, I wasn't forced to acknowledge all the falsities in my unworthy picture of myself.

I think deep down I believed I was a good person, but I could never truly see what others saw. This meant that when it came to the crunch in those very hard times, I had nothing to hold onto, nothing "worthy" to call upon within me and get me out of that place.

That's when I realised I needed to take action and start looking at myself in a whole new light. If those who loved me could see beautiful qualities in me then why couldn't I see and believe in them too?

I found the exercise of creating an *I am Worthy* list extremely helpful and uplifting, and I still call upon those words on that list to this day.

I want you to create your own *I am Worthy* list. Choose three people in your life whom you hold dear. These are the people who know you best, who you trust the most, and whose opinions you respect. Ask each of them to give you three positive words that describe you best.

This will challenge you; most of us are humble by nature and don't like seeking out compliments. You may feel surprised, you may disagree but you will find a common thread amongst them.

Make a note of the words you are given. Write them on sticky notes and place them around the house or set them as reminders on your phone or computer.

Every time you have a moment when you are thinking about jumping on the self-sabotage train with its clunking carriages of unworthiness and judgement, remember this list. Go to it. Read it. Know deep down in your core that these words are part of you. Someone who loves you just as you are sees these qualities in you.

Believe the words and repeat them to yourself. Repetition creates new patterns. Our brains believed the stories we kept reinforcing over the years, so this no different, except it is way more positive and fuelled by love.

Keep reading that list and believe every letter in every word. You are those words. You embody those qualities.

After you shed some tears of gratitude and love, your ego will resist these words. Thoughts will arise that they are just being nice because you asked, but remember, you asked people who love you already to simply verbalise with you how they feel about you and what they see that you can't yet.

We aren't always the best at telling those we care for what they truly mean to us, so this can be a new experience for both parties.

Just because this may be the first time you have heard these words, does not take away their validity. They are saying them because they are true.

To take this little love fest to the next level, return the favour. Pay it forward and say three nice things that you love or admire about them... better yet, do this little exercise with your kids.

If you still need some encouragement to quieten the whispers of doubt, keep in mind this thought from Vincent van Gogh: 'If you hear a voice within you say "You cannot paint", then by all means paint and that voice will be silenced.'

The same applies to your belief in yourself. Believe it and it will be true.

The light

Some days I can see what's real from what I think is real; when I know in my heart whether I'm doing alright or I'm buying into the bullshit. Today I questioned myself incessantly and sat side-by-side with the bullshit. Not only did I sit with it, I was swallowed by it. It's bizarre how I can find comfort in something that actually takes me further away from my truth. It's easy to keep going on the path of the self created story, believe the lies about my worth, and remain ignorant to the truth that is waiting to be seen. And it's much easier today to believe I wasn't meant for this job of being a mum. I remember wondering if I ever would be a mum despite having so much love inside to give. Spooner said I was a natural. I wasn't convinced, probably still am not. But what I would give to be that woman he once saw. To feel like I'm meant to be here and doing this motherhood thing. When people say it is going to be hard, they don't talk about this – the doubt, the questioning, the destruction and the helplessness. My world is always mad, crazy and noisy, and most of the time I feel I'm in the eye of the tornado, separate from it all but knowing I'm about to be swept up. From the outside maybe I seem like I have it together, or maybe I look like I'm losing grip, barely hanging on to a thread of hope. But as long as there is that I hope, I will never once loosen my grip. I've worked so hard to get to this point, even if all I have are glimpses of the truth of who I am. Just please, keep giving me these little glimpses to keep me going.

We have covered some complex emotional issues and core feelings that most, well let's be real here, all mothers will feel at some point in time.

It may be that some of what you have read and reflected upon or so far has revealed certain things to you that make you feel a bit uncomfortable, perhaps it was so uncomfortable it was palpable.

Perhaps you have a better idea now of where some of the challenges in your life arise.

You might be sensing some resentment and feeling the impulse to lay blame. It's in all of us to do this. Holding that blame is heavy and we need to place it down somewhere.

We don't want to admit weakness or defeat because we associate these with failure, and no one wants to be a failure. So instead, we deflect the responsibility of our lives onto the circumstances or people around us. We wonder why certain things happen to us and how we could possibly deserve them.

I'm sure we can all admit that we've had a *Why me?* moment while looking up to the heavens for answers. Our ego loves to let us fall into the mindset of being a victim. This is the place where all our fears live and can easily thrive.

To be a victim implies disengagement and detachment from what is occurring. It means we don't have to take responsibility for the circumstances in our lives because we feel that we are not answerable for what is happening to us.

I'm sorry, but I'm not prepared to let you hide behind that lie anymore. Part of your journey towards grace and strength as a mother means facing up to the false stories, forgiving yourself and making a choice about how you want to live. Only when you do this can you move beyond fear and finally step into the light.

Taking ownership

As it transpires, one of the most confronting lessons yet the biggest growth you will experience is to accept that you are responsible for your own life.

Now this responsibility has nothing to do with deserving it or not. That is irrelevant. The reason I am responsible for my current circumstance is that all of my actions have led me to this point.

Some of you reading these words may want to reject this idea. You might feel uncomfortable, even angry, or wronged by the implication that you are somehow to blame for your situation.

But there is no blame needed here at all. The past is the past. Decisions were made. Sometimes it's even just the lack of a decision that brings us into this space of learning. One thing I know for sure is, we are forever learning and getting better each day.

Your ego is either going to say *No way is all of this crap that is happening my fault, I never asked for this and I don't deserve this stress in my life!* or it might be telling you *Yes, actually I am totally to blame for everything, it's all my fault,* and you can then slide right down on your self-hatred spiral.

Regardless of which of these stories plays in your mind, I'm here to tell you the story you should be letting sink into your heart – **I am the only person fully responsible for my own life. I take full ownership of my sovereignty and my life.**

Could there be anything more empowering than when we take ownership of everything back into ourselves? When we know that each decision is ours to make, that each moment we can choose. To know that we have the power to direct our lives in the way we want. To even know that all the pain and hurt that has been done to us can be ours to take ownership of, incorporate into our new knowing and heal so the power lies with us and not those who caused us pain.

Accepting responsibility for where we are in our lives is actually an incredibly empowering act. It can be a painful process to acknowledge that our decisions in life have led us to this point and may have created the very unease we are currently experiencing.

Working through the resistance associated with acceptance takes time, and I'm not going to sugar-coat that. It will be hard and sometimes painful. There will be resistance but recognising the role we play in our circumstances gives us the power to make changes.

Throughout my lifetime, my compromised sense of self has led me straight into relationships and situations that would bring this life lesson to the surface.

I had relationships in my earlier years that reinforced my lack of self-worth. It's like I was seeking out those who would reinforce the false stories I had been believing about myself. I was attracting people to prove to me I wasn't deserving of better than this.

By not standing up for what I believed to be true about myself, and by letting other people call me names and put me down I reinforced all the negative stories I had created about myself in my head.

My ego and my cooperation with it got me deep into a place where I couldn't love myself and couldn't be with people who truly loved me either. That place can feel very dark and lonely and those feelings don't always stay behind in those relationships when we have left. Leaving relationships or avoiding situations doesn't clear the stories and beliefs, they are still within until they are witnessed and healed.

Releasing the past

Suffering is not holding you. You are holding suffering. When you become good at the art of letting sufferings go, then you'll come to realize how unnecessary it was for you to drag those burdens around with you. You'll see that no one else other than you was responsible. The truth is that existence wants your life to become a festival.

— OSHO

When you are on a journey of self-discovery like the one you have embarked upon, your driving force is about ending up in a place that feels like home. It's about moulding and shaping a better, brighter future, and part of moving towards that light involves releasing the darkness in your past.

We all have a lifetime of moments, decisions and experiences that shape the very version of ourselves that we are today. With reflection we can sometimes see that the pain and suffering, the confusion, the bad decisions, the toxic relationships and even the regrets all had their place. An amazing tapestry of perfection in some ways, leading us to shed all of that and become more grounded within our truest self than before.

The happy moments alongside these harder moments are not who you are, they do not define you; it is the decisions you make afterwards. It is the changes and realisations you have after that define who you are.

You are not your mistakes or errors in judgement, you are all the things you do afterwards.

I love the quote from Maya Angelou: 'Do the best you can until you know better. Then when you know better, do better.'

I don't want you to go thinking that this process of letting go is another opportunity to feel shame or frustration with yourself. The process of living a human existence is to iron out all these prickly edges and living through it is the only way to learn. Instead, it's a case of acknowledging that within you lies the power to let go of all those unhelpful, restrictive feelings that have affected the way you define your worthiness.

Sadly, experiencing some form of trauma in our lives is far too common. We can be in a state of trauma from incidents in the playground at school or the way a parent's tone hurt our feelings, to deeper sufferings such as childhood abuse or trauma, enduring a toxic relationship, being emotionally abandoned by family, or losing a loved one.

I am not qualified in trauma therapy or psychology so we won't go deeper into how these experiences can affect us, but I encourage you to reach out to a qualified health professional if you need support.

I will never downplay the impact of these experiences in our lives but what I want to focus on is how we can take control. The point I'm gently trying to make here is that I am aware of how your past pain can feel like something that has been done to you, but that right now, in this moment, you have the power to not let your past control your future.

I'm not saying you shouldn't feel like life has not always been kind to you. I'm not saying you haven't been through some very difficult times. I'm not even saying that you weren't a victim. All I am asking is that you open yourself to the possibility of not letting the events of your past define you into the future.

During my twenties, I had a long relationship of the kind that is typical of many youthful relationships. We shared common interests in music and social events, had a great time together and genuinely did love each other. But with that love and time came a level of comfort that allowed me to blur my own boundaries.

My unclear lines around what I was willing to accept, combined with my own crippling sense of self-worth, enabled my partner to emotionally use me. He had struggled for years with panic disorder and anxiety and I felt I did all I could to help him work through that. Yet when people aren't in control of their own lives, they feel the need to control others.

In my lack of inner strength, I helped him create a victim out of me. I allowed my life to be controlled.

Over time, in between moments of love, it became an emotionally abusive relationship. He called me fat, worthless and stupid. He did his best to keep me insecure and in my place. We had replaced our loving environment with a toxic relationship that didn't serve either of us in being our best version of ourselves. I think we had both completely lost the essence of who we were.

It has taken me some time to detach from how soul-crushing that period in my life was for me. I could very easily have stayed attached to it and continued to blame him for how his behaviour created my insecurities, trust issues and defensiveness. I could continue to blame myself for my own actions, for being weak and not standing up for myself and being more honest about my feelings. But I couldn't change the past. I couldn't change what we had both already done to one another. And we had both acted out of pain.

With time I've forgiven both of us, because I realised that the longer I let that part of my life define my worthiness, the more I was giving power to the negative and choosing fear rather than love.

In the end, this is a story that I didn't want to associate with any longer. I cannot lay claim to his behaviour, for that is a demon he has to make peace with himself, but I had to make peace with the fact that I allowed myself to be a victim.

At the time, I felt safe in playing that role, and understandably so. It is easy to get caught up in that victim mentality when the voice of courage within you has been shushed for too long.

The relationships we have, especially with those closest to us, always act as a mirror. They will reflect back to us what we need to address within ourselves.

Every experience has a lesson. Yet all experiences in the past also need to be let go at some point.

Your past experiences and behaviour do not define you; every moment after that, every other decision you make in courage is what defines you.

The gift in adversity

I remember the drive home from the appointment. Looking out the window at the bush landscape around us. Wanting to say something but not knowing how to make all those thoughts and feelings come out of my mouth.

Was there ever going to be a way I could articulate what was inside me right now?

"I can tell you that after these assessments and working with your son Harry, that he has Autism Spectrum Disorder." The words kind of floated out of her mouth. It didn't hit me hard, it was like it just floated in the space between us waiting for me to take it all in.

There wasn't shock and denial for me. My gut was telling me for a long time that there was something we were missing with Harry.

Despite everyone reassuring us he was young, he would talk soon, he is just frustrated and so on… there was always something inside me that knew he wasn't a happy little boy. He was distant at times. Disconnected from us. As his mama I felt a barrier I couldn't quite explain between us. I could feel the love inside this little boy but it was like he couldn't access it at times. He seemed trapped in his own little world.

Harry's Autism diagnosis felt like a relief. It was the piece of the puzzle that reassured me I wasn't failing as his mother. That all of our struggles together were likely because of an element out of our control.

The biggest relief by far was having answers so we could now give Harry the support he needed. So we could start understanding him in a way we struggled to during those early years. To finally know our little

Harry as we had yet to know him.

Having a child diagnosed with Autism is a unique experience for every family. This can be shattering for some, hard to accept, painful and scary. Every experience is unique and right. Having any kind of news that makes you reflect on the life your child may have in the future is going to strike deep into your heart.

There have been many days when I wonder what adult life may look like for Harry and Jacob (years later we also discovered that Jacob too had Autism and Attention Deficit Hyperactivity Disorder). How they will navigate all of this. What will school be like for them? Will they have relationships and be able to hold a job? The unknowns about the future are perhaps the hardest.

We want the best for our kids, nothing short of it, and when there is a chance something may derail that then we almost panic inside. We don't know how to do this if we can't protect them from the world. We search for the good, desperately needing to know that within this adversity our children will be okay, that we all will be okay.

We've all heard it before: in every cloud there is a silver lining. Much as we might like to deny it, it's one of those things where it's a cliché because it's true.

Sometimes that lining is easy to perceive. At other times, we may feel that we will never understand what we are supposed to take from our moment of adversity.

All of us mothers face many such moments every single day. They can be fleeting, like when a toddler has a hissy fit in the middle of the supermarket, or they might linger around longer, as with health scares, financial pressures or emotional breakdowns.

In times like these we often ask ourselves why. We can feel victimised by our struggles and be weakened to the point where we feel helpless.

But it is when we get to that point of helplessness, the lonely and scary place that is our rock bottom, that we have the opportunity to welcome back some light.

In the midst of such desperation, we search all the more deeply for that truth within and it becomes possible to acknowledge that this may be happening for a reason. If we can recognise the divine perfection of these events, we can start to invite light back into our lives and begin the journey of moving forward with new information and a clearer resolution about ourselves and where we want to be, both spiritually and physically.

Being brought to our knees usually gives us a whole new perspective on life. It's only when you are here that you can see the way back up.

In the process of trying to evaluate how to make it all better, we are often compelled to start peeling back the layers and digging deeper into ourselves. We develop greater self-awareness and reflection is easier to access.

That's certainly how it happened for me. I probably could have continued on with a lifetime of self-destructive, mum-hating talk to myself if my depression and anxiety had not forced me to readdress the way I approach my entire life.

I look back over the years and think we have endured too much adversity. We have lost a baby, lost loved ones, said goodbye to many homes, navigated children with special needs and endured many years of mental health issues. It hasn't been easy. But every single bit of it made me who I am today.

I may wonder what life would be like if some of these harder times never happened, and sure, my heart longs for the memories I lost when I was deeply depressed or to hold my mum's hand again or to see our boys not have to struggle every day with basic things. That wonder comes from a place of love. A desire to fill those places in my heart that feel broken or like a void that may never be filled.

I'm learning to accept that I can have this wonder and longing and also know that everything happened exactly as it should.

One thing I said to myself through all the years of challenges is that I would never be given any challenge I cannot handle. And it's true. You will only ever be given that which you can rise above.

Choosing love over fear

Love is the relationship between you and your partner. It is the bond you have with your children, the connection you have with your family and the ties that bind you and your friends. It's also found in the companionship you have with a pet and it is the source of all your passions in life.

Love is all of these things, but it is also a way to live your life.

Indeed, the only life intended for us is one of love. This encompasses how you live your life, how you respond to what happens within you and around you, how you interact with others and the impact you leave on this world.

Fear, quite simply, is all the things that block love.

Love is...

oneness, acceptance, authenticity, compassion, endearment, understanding, forgiveness, gratitude, empathy, unity, passion, generosity, faithfulness, optimism, honesty, soulfulness, inclusivity, curiosity, courage, helpfulness and grace.

Fear is...

judgement, comparison, competition, entitlement, envy, resentment, denial, ignorance, dramatising, negativity, unawareness, pessimism, spitefulness, malice, failure, defeat, cynicism, doubt, exclusivity, and resistance.

In each moment in our life when we are faced with a decision on which path we shall take, we choose our response.

When someone treats us poorly, we have every right to be hurt, but when we choose to resent that person, we are siding with fear when we could instead choose forgiveness.

When we analyse ourselves for being a crappy mummy, we can choose a fearful response and judge ourselves harshly or decide on a loving response and practise compassion towards ourselves.

Making the choice of love over fear does not mean you are not entitled to feel certain emotions; as you've probably worked out already, I am all in favour of feeling your feelings. But by choosing a more loving response, you can pave the way for healing.

If someone does wrong by me, I let myself be angry at them for however long I need without any expectation. I am allowed to feel anger if I have been wronged or triggered by someone's actions or words. I don't dwell in this space but I let my feelings be what they need to be until I feel ready. Then I choose a loving response. It may look like forgiveness or letting it go because this situation needs compassion.

At times we may not feel like others deserve these things from us, but often their behaviour has nothing at all to do with us and everything to do with them.

I always say to our kids if someone is saying things you don't like or being mean to you or one of your friends, it is usually because they have big feelings inside themselves they don't know what to do with. It really is less about us and more about them. Yet in the same breath others are also the greatest mirror to within ourselves and our barriers to love.

When I have a tough day with the kids, I usually begin on my downward spiral of self-loathing, judgement and criticism. It's on autopilot most of the time, but my awareness is getting more fine-tuned to this every single day.

I can side with fear and feed all the stories that block love coming back to me or I can choose to see love instead. I no longer see my day or myself as a failure. With loving eyes, I can see that I am a great mama who is doing a pretty good job most days of the week. I become realistic, accepting and much more forgiving.

Choosing love gives me the power to turn around my mood.

I choose to see love instead
I choose to see love instead
I choose to see love instead

Whenever you're faced with uncomfortable feelings or experiences like these, choose love. When someone hurts you, choose love. When you're trapped in angst in your own head, choose love. When you're riding the self-attacking train, always choose love.

This is not a case of you taking the high road, because the result will benefit you just as much as anyone else.

Throughout this book we get into some of the big issues that hold all of us mums in a place of fear. Whenever something tough like that comes up, just keep choosing love.

It takes some practise to lean into love and change the negative messages in your head, but it is vital that you start doing this.

Fear will always keep you from expanding and embracing the essence of who you are. Love, on the other hand, lets you see how amazing you really are. It recognises the good work you are doing, allows you to make mistakes (because you are human, after all), and encourages you to keep going.

Love will remind you of the essence of who you are.

Changing your
internal dialogue

Our own inner critic is the harshest of all. More often than not we would not speak to anyone else in the same way we are able to speak to ourselves. We are our own judges and executors.

This voice is our ego, the one trying to keep us blocked from love.

Our ego can block us from love, but it is also showing us incredible guideposts to what we need to heal. When we hear our ego voice rattling off all the hurtful untruths about ourselves, it's actually showing us the things we need to heal most.

You're doing a terrible job.

Clearly you were just never cut out to be a mother.

You really are just not good enough.

You're useless, why can't you get it together?

What's wrong with you anyway? Why are you so hopeless?

You should just give up.

How long do you think you can keep pretending like this?

Our problem? We believe all our thoughts. My psychologist once said "Just because you think that, does not make it true."

We are not useless, weak and not good enough. These are *symptoms of not living your truth*, putting everyone else before you and not being connected to your inner self.

Our thoughts are powerful. Our brain does not actually know reality from a fictitious story we tell it. If we feed our brains with self-limiting stories about ourselves, we start to believe it.

How do you speak to yourself in your mind? Is it with loving reassurance, kindness and empathy? Or is there disdain, judgement and cruelty in your tone?

To embody all the things we want to be, it all starts within. How you speak to yourself is the foundation of self-love.

You can buy the most beautiful dress with heels and earrings but if you don't tell yourself you are beautiful then you won't feel beautiful.

My anxiety is the worst culprit for feeding my inner critic. When you have anxiety it's like your mind never stops, it is constantly thinking, processing and analysing something, anything. Eventually you run out of stuff to worry about and turn on yourself.

I've always struggled with my own self-worth and so my inner critic speaks pretty loud to me most of the time. I haven't banished her, but I'm much more aware when it's my ego talking. I remind myself that my thoughts are not always my truth. I know I am much greater and more wonderful than that.

That's not arrogant, I just know I'm bigger than all that. And deep down you do too.

Sometimes the overwhelm in our lives will lead us to believe any story we are fed as our insecurities try desperately to latch onto another part of ourselves. But inside us we all know our truth. It's always there. We were born with our own perfection and divinity programmed into our DNA. I believe our life's mission is to spend our time here trying to uncover all the things that block us from embodying that divinity. To have the realisation of who we are and how perfect our existence actually is.

We are far greater than any nasty comments to ourselves. Those comments can be our stepping stones to finding the inner knowing of our divinity.

There is power in all our words both internal and external. As much as a nasty comment will hurt someone else's feelings, nasty words from your inner critic will do the same to you.

There was an experiment done by Japanese author and Pseudo scientist Doctor Masaru Emoto about the effects of words and how they can actually change matter. He had jars of water all from the same source, and each jar was labelled with an emotion. There were anger, rage, war, joy, love and prayer to name a few.

They spoke words to the water and treated it in correspondence with the word on their label for long periods of time. When they analysed the water under a microscope all had a different makeup. The water particles had changed shape.

The water that was subjected to loving words had beautiful patterns resembling snowflakes. The water that had been subjected to negative and fear-based words was broken, jagged and visually disturbed.

The words changed the water. The words had power.

If we speak to ourselves with negativity for long enough, we may not just believe what we say but we could potentially have a negative impact on our own health and wellbeing.

The more you become aware of your internal critic and the times when your dialogue is not loving and supportive, the easier it becomes to see through it all.

Next time that negative internal dialogue starts up, try following these steps:

---

1. **Acknowledge the language of your inner critic**
    You will find there are certain words, phrases and names

that reappear when you speak to yourself. Start to witness the pattern that forms.

2. **Take a step back and see the situation for what it really is**
   Ask the questions... *Am I really a bad mother right now? Does my body deserve me to hate it so much?* et cetera.

3. **Rephrase the message with love and reassure yourself with kindness**
   Find something loving to say to yourself. Every time you choose love, it counts. It makes a difference in how you feel.

Just recently I purchased our boys a journal for them to write all their experiences in. It is a prompted journal that talks about positive self-image, being your own ambassador and gratitude.

Our eldest, Jacob, is a beautifully sensitive boy who at this point in his life, struggles with his own self-belief. On a daily basis this amazing boy goes to school and manages to get through the day with Autism, ADHD and Dyslexia accompanying him. That cocktail makes school pretty hard for him on most days.

When he excitedly grabbed his new journal to start filling it out, I could see his excitement turn to sadness.

He didn't tick many of the boxes on the page outlining his superpowers. He didn't believe he could make friends, that his brain was powerful, that he could learn anything and do great things.

My heart smashed into a thousand pieces and it took all my might to hold back the tears.

My baby was sad inside and didn't love himself enough to see all the things that we see in him. His challenges in life were overshadowing all his amazing capabilities.

Seeing this in him reminded me of how important our internal dialogue is. How can I teach my children to love themselves and believe in themselves if I don't do the same for me?

We sat together and spoke about all the boxes he left unticked, some even had dark heavy crosses in them just so we were all aware of all the things he couldn't do. We read them out loud, my heart piercing with each one. Then I asked him questions that prompted him to rethink his answers.

I helped him reflect on himself, to look within and find that inner knowing of his own awesomeness.

He was shaky, admittedly, but he started to smile. It feels nice to hear nice things about yourself... especially when you really do believe it inside.

Living in your authenticity

The privilege of a lifetime is to become who you truly are.
— CARL JUNG

Ruby, our youngest, is everything I could have been. She has all the strong traits and follow-through that the bewildered child in me lost over time.

She is only four, but when you have a child like this one you will know exactly what I am talking about.

It may be stubbornness, sass and feistiness, you can call it all of that, which I often do too, but I can see that fire in her comes from strength. An inner knowing of what she wants and won't accept any other way.

She is our last child so I'm sure I've softened to her in a way I didn't with the boys, part of it may be me giving in and picking my battles more often.

But it's also something else. I have this feeling like she will never apologise for who she is.

She is Scorpio just like her father and if you know anything about horoscopes you know I've got my work cut out for me. She challenges everything in me. She is difficult and loving in one breath. One moment she adores me, the next I'm never her best friend again.

I don't want to change her though. I want her to keep all of this and refine it into a graceful power when she is older. I want her to be a strong woman who knows herself so well she won't take anything less from another soul.

As parents I think we fall into the trap of wanting to shape our kids into what we want them to be. We resist against their inner power and try to tame them so it's more comfortable and easier for us.

Our little sunflower, as Daddy calls her, has shown me that despite how much she challenges me I can't change her.

I've spent most of my life trying to undo all the restrictive beliefs I have adopted about myself. I can't let her run that same path.

She will have her own journey and challenges, but that inner fire that she already has is not what I want to take from her.

When you watch children, you see their authenticity. When they are young, they haven't quite worked out that everyone is actually different. They are finding their feet in the social world. They just are who they are.

From everything you've read of my story so far, you'll know it's safe to say I've never been an overly confident person and have always been way too easily swayed by the opinions of others. I've spent most of my life striving to be something I'm not, which has ultimately left me on a search for something I was never going to find – a version of myself that never existed.

Instead of searching for the real me, seeking to live a full, honest and deeply connected life in the true essence of who I am, I kept being pulled to and fro by my yearning to be accepted and to fit in.

There were times when I drank too much alcohol in the mistaken belief that it was the only way I could feel confident, let loose and have a good time. There were times I beat myself up because I didn't look the same as that super-fit pregnant woman who was sporting a perfect baby bump. There are still times when I shy away from speaking my truth because I feel others don't understand or value my opinion.

Each one of those times has taken me a step further away from my authentic self. I have actively chosen to turn my back on my authenticity because I believed the only way to feel happy and content was by ticking all the boxes of being everyone else's idea of what an acceptable version of me was.

I spent so long looking, striving and hoping, but ultimately ignoring my truest self that was right before me.

I was so focused on fitting in because, in the end, isn't that what we all search for in our teen years and beyond? A way to feel socially accepted and find our people.

We want to be accepted and loved at our core. But to do so we trade ourselves to make it work. We have come to believe that being accepted is more important than being ourselves.

I could regret all the time I spent trying to find a way to fit in, but what I've come to realise is that we keep on searching until we know what it is we are truly looking for. We may not even realise we are lost until one moment changes it all for us.

Some of us, like my Rubes, may be pretty set in our understanding of who we are and what makes us tick, we know ourselves so well. Some of us, more like me, are lost after many years of trying to fill that void with something else.

Are any of us able to live in our authenticity, unjaded by the world around us?

We will all have moments when the world tries to dim that light within us. Our response is to start on the search again.

Our life lessons are wise and welcome in people, relationships and experiences that will force us to remain connected to ourselves, to be reminded of our authenticity and then to choose if we will live authentically or be dimmed again.

This is particularly true when we become parents. How easily as mums are we distracted by all the things we "should" be doing?

These are things that get drilled into us at antenatal classes, at midwife appointments and doctor's visits, during mothers' groups, and from television and social media.

This list of "should" is endless, so it's no wonder that we keep stepping away from our authenticity and questioning what we think and believe.

We listen to what we are told, not what we know.

But time is on our side. I feel that the older we get, the more honest we become about who we are, and the more we learn that we don't need to apologise for any of it.

When you are living in authenticity, there is no need for any competition. You no longer have to worry about what anyone else is doing, thinking or saying, because the only thing that matters is you. Authenticity is so beautiful because it is so real.

I'm not drawn to "perfect" people, they make me paranoid and quite honestly, they are boring to me. Give me quirks, radical laughter and crazy tears. Give me the woman who is real and refuses to put up a facade just so I'll like her more. I like everyone more when they are themselves.

I've given up trying to be someone I'm not. I'm emotional, stubborn and too trusting. I find it hard to ask for help. I'm lazy when it comes to cleaning. I'm a bookworm and fascinated by learning anything new. I can't tell a joke to save my life. I'm a tree- and animal-loving tripper. I cry a lot and that feels healthy to me. I'm almost always running late. I won't buy into gossip. I have a spiritual side and adore anything mystical. The drama of reality TV shows irks me. I have a real body that birthed three babies and I'm learning every day to love it more.

That's me, authentic and bare. I hope my children grow up knowing these things and all the other quirks and imperfections that are me.

In truth, I wouldn't want them to know me any other way.

Part II

Reconnection

Returning

Who am I anymore? The heaviness of that question weighs on me each and every day. It's a difficult balance of seeking the answer to who I am and who I think I've become. The becoming part is laced with guilt. I feel like I've lost myself but does that mean I don't love being a mum or that I don't love this new life we have created? In my heart of hearts, I know that's not the case, but the guilt lingers nevertheless. Can I have both? Can I still feel connected but be okay with what I've lost? I hope so. Why do I feel like I have lost something when I have gained so much? Pouring my soul and love into being a mum is what I have always wanted. I longed for a family and it just felt natural to me, but I never anticipated this feeling. It's like a scratching at my heart when I'm neck-deep in crazy-mum-land and all I want is out, yet the longing to just be there and love my babes is always present too. God, the guilt is debilitating! I guess I'm supposed to just become a mum and be happy with all that entails, even if it means I lose a piece of myself, but I'm resisting that loss. I wonder if other mums feel that same loss, that guilt and that scratching at their heart? It's like being torn between two worlds. Is it possible to live in both worlds? Better yet to thrive in two worlds? That feels like the most far away possibility for me. I want so desperately to be the woman I was. I know I've grown but I'm also so lost. The reality is nothing will change, being a mother is my life. And I love my life... but in those harder perhaps weaker moments, or even just in the silence I'm always looking for myself. I guess I'll just have to live with the guilt of grieving for the woman I used to know.

Welcome back, Sweetheart. In this part of the book, we are going to start delving into the beautiful rediscovery of you.

I say rediscovery because this is the thing about being a mum – we lose ourselves in it. We throw ourselves so deeply and lovingly into the world of raising our children that who we are, what we stand for and what our soul yearns for can get set aside. But the thing to remember is that these qualities are never truly lost. Everything that shines so brightly about you is still there. You just need a reminder sometimes of what speaks to your heart and how incredible you are.

You can have both – motherhood and self-connection. It is truly possible to live authentically in your new world as a mother.

I want you to find that connection with you, the girl you know deep in your heart, the one whose voice only you can hear. She is the essence of you who over time, through the initiations of motherhood, has been lost.

She is the one who doesn't change her will or make decisions out of fear of judgement. She lives fully in herself and in her authenticity, which is brilliant, because despite what you may think, nobody wants a filtered or fake version of you. I know in your heart that you don't want that either.

Reconnection gives you a beautiful opportunity to come back to who you are, love yourself in all your magnificence and share yourself joyfully with others.

Losing yourself

It usually starts for me with the 3am wake-up cry. When it happens again at 4am, I am usually the one who's crying from exhaustion and/or frustration and debating whether it's time for milk or if that decision will just shoot me in the foot later on.

Once everyone has risen for the day, the breakfast cereal gets spilt all over the floor and a delivery arrives when I'm in the midst of changing the dirtiest of nappies. When I finally sit down for a much-needed cup of tea, a tantrum erupts for, well, let's be honest, who knows what reason? And all of this takes place before 9am.

For all you mamas of little ones, I bet this is an all too familiar morning. Outside the daily challenges of being a mum, we can find that everything just seems a little out of whack all at the same time.

Balance is elusive in motherhood and it is all spanning across many aspects of our lives. Our fitness may be non-existent, we have been snapping at our partner, we find ourselves snacking (or gorging) on all the wrong but oh-so-right foods, we are tired and fatigued, the bills just keep piling up, things are way too busy at work, the kid's behaviour is off, or they keep getting sick–and all of it is going on together.

This is the reality of motherhood and trying to find balance between woman, mother, wife, self. That often takes years for many of us. I think we need to arrive at a space where we know we are at (or close to) breaking point to really shift gears and make some changes.

Perhaps we have to be stripped back to our basics. Perhaps losing ourselves in all of this is exactly what we need to fully understand the value of our own self. To appreciate ourselves for who we are. To value ourselves so much we will stand up and be strong when we or our children are wronged.

Is this disconnection and shedding of our old self the perfect conditions for us to be reborn? To connect with our truest self that was perhaps lost even before our children were born. The shedding makes way for our truest self to come forth and for the lessons that motherhood imparts on us to have space to be held.

Motherhood has changed me in ways I never thought possible. It has shown me life through a lens that is more beautiful than I could imagine. It has shown me I am stronger than I ever knew I could be.

When we become mothers everything else falls away for a time, and that is normal. To love, nurture and care for our babies when they first arrive requires a selfless devotion that is instinctual. But for many of us, the line of transition is blurred and we just continue on this devotion in a way that isn't healthy for our own identity and sense of self.

I'm not even sure we can avoid this process, or should. Like I said I believe it could be the modern rite of passage into motherhood. It isn't anything you have done wrong and you haven't let yourself down – this is the reality of motherhood in this age.

Part of the greatest challenge is that even when we have awareness of this disconnect from ourselves – a frustration at being a mother and a desire to find what's missing within – we don't actually have a lot of space to work through those feelings.

Motherhood is busy. If we can't manage to pee by ourselves, we are for sure going to struggle to do deep soul-searching work.

And trust me, I've been on my own process of self-growth and awakening for years and kids and awakenings don't mix too well.

Finding the space to sit with our feelings and really get intimate with them, understand them and have the capacity to make changes takes commitment and sometimes, that level of commitment from us is too much. It's just one more thing to add to our plate.

Let's face it, finding yourself again is not like a gentle walk in the park. It requires you to face your shadows, speak up for your needs, set boundaries you may have never set before and be willing for some things to burn so that there is space for newness.

So how do mamas do the work? How do we find ourselves again amongst all the beautiful madness of motherhood? We acknowledge that living our life disconnected from our truest self is way more painful than the process of letting everything that does not work burn down.

A life lived without authenticity and self-awareness is like being trapped. Some of you may already feel trapped and, my love, you deserve so much more than this.

A cascade of events happens not because the world is out to get you, but because you're out of alignment with yourself. The more dramatic your life feels, the further away you are from where you should be.

That's when you need to pause and reflect.

Are you being true to yourself?
Are you standing in your power?
Are you living your life with authenticity?
Are you looking after yourself physically and emotionally?

When life throws a few too many crazy days or weeks at you and it seems like it's just one thing after another, this is often a sign that the Universe is giving you a little tap on the shoulder to tell you it's time to make a shift.

When this beautiful madness of motherhood leads us to feel we have lost touch with ourselves, our relationships or our dreams – the only way to get back in touch is through an authentic reconnection with ourselves. Which means remembering who you are and what you love about yourself and for yourself, which is you, mama, step-mama, wife, friend, sister, daughter... all of these elements make up you.

We all know this, but as I've said, the all-consuming bubble of mother-land can make us fall into the trap that being mum comes before absolutely everything. But with this there is no balance.

I've let go of the guilt of feeling like I don't have to put myself aside anymore. Because the key here is harmony. The story that my children can only thrive when I am depleted is wrong. It never could be right.

Being a mum does not require you to sacrifice all that you believe in and love, to sacrifice your wants, to let go of your health and let everyone else come before you. This won't last, this story will break you down like it has and will do to too many of us mothers.

Without you being a happy and content mother who is connected to herself, your children won't be happy either and they will lack the role model they need you to be.

This time with our kids is precious, I'm speaking from my perspective as a mama to three little ones. They actually still want to be with me, they still have sweet-sounding voices with innocent (and hilarious) questions, they still love snuggles on the lounge and story time. But as they grow, I know these moments will change.

For so many years I had shattered pieces of my heart looking to be mended, the parts of me devastated that perhaps I've lost this precious time with them. That perhaps my mental health issues and my disconnection from self had made me distant when I should have been so near.

Devastatingly, some of that likely is true. But I will not let this continue on. I want to be fully connected into my heart and happy within myself and my life so that I can be present for them.

I knew I had to find myself, there wasn't any other option.

Finding yourself

Do you even remember the stuff you loved to do before parenting and its demands came along? Sometimes I really have to think to remember what I did before I had kids. I always thought I was busy, but now I wonder what exactly I was busy with.

Spooner and I often joke about this. What did we do with all our free time?

We did whatever we wanted to, actually. We filled space spending time with those we loved and doing things that made our hearts full.

We have to and want to make space for our little ones when they arrive and over time, when their needs from us soften a little, we do have the space to start welcoming more of what makes us fulfilled outside of parenthood back into our lives.

If we don't actively choose to do more of the things we love at any stage of motherhood, we will always feel lost.

Being a parent is deeply fulfilling like nothing else, but there are so many aspects to ourselves and we can't fill all of those needs through parenting.

Whether it was going for a walk or doing a workout at the gym, sitting down to enjoy the next chapter of your favourite book, beers with friends, staying up way too late bingeing on movies (hell, even going to a cinema!) or having a lazy afternoon nap, whatever you loved, you did.

Being a parent means that time for doing this stuff can get complicated and engaging in even the simplest of activities can become an all-out event requiring drop-off plans, car seat switches and a nappy bag equipped for Armageddon.

It's easy to understand how the required compromise of parenting can become a much bigger issue when we don't have enough of the other things in life happening alongside parenting. It's a slow progression of losing our connection with ourselves that happens naturally when we give all we have to our beautiful family, but this pure devotion often leaves us forgetting who we are when we are not a mum or wife or partner.

But no single role defines who we are as a person. We are all a complex tapestry of longings and desires. Switching them off for a time will work but the inner calling for something that is a part of you will eventually arise. It may whisper or it could be a roar that feels like frustration and resentment.

I'm going to say to you directly that being a mother is an important role we play in life, but it is definitely not the only one and we don't have to sacrifice everything in order to be a good mum. Who are you outside of being a mother?

Finding yourself again isn't just about doing activities you love, that's the easy part actually. Finding yourself is understanding all the things that have changed about you.

Like we talked about, motherhood changes you in the most profound of ways. In some ways it feels like finding your old self and finding your new self and merging the two together.

We may turn off our connection to ourselves because it can be easier to be numb, to float, to do as expected and not create waves. Finding yourself can make big waves. Within yourself and for those around you.

Not everyone may agree with the "new" you, they may feel challenged by your new confidence, new opinions or change of lifestyle. And they can feel that way all they want, because this life is not theirs to live – it is yours.

Even the people closest to us can feel intimidated or challenged by us stepping into ourselves and finding ourselves again and often it is because for you to make change it means the world changes around you. Creating more space for yourself may mean you have stronger boundaries and are less available to others than you were in the past.

Your new inner knowing may mean you take less crap from others and push back in negative or toxic situations.

People aren't bad for disliking your change, they just have enjoyed the comfort of the way things have always been. But when you find yourself again you will also find your people. Those that accept all of you as you are.

Finding ourselves takes some deep exploration and a willingness to look at our shadows. To see those parts of ourselves we have often kept hidden. It means we need to be willing to stop following the acceptable archetype of a mother and a woman and do what feels good inside our cells.

We often feel like we are searching for an elusive, intangible feeling, this thing we don't fully understand but can *just feel*. Maybe it's the search for self or maybe it's the reconnection with the truth that is already within.

We haven't forgotten who we are. We are the wisdom keepers of ourselves and that won't ever change.

I am my own wisdom keeper.
To find myself I simply need to pause and
listen within.

I'm forever finding myself and maybe losing myself again on a cycle of repeat. But now that I have reconnected and found myself, I know that feeling. I know what I need and desire outside of motherhood, it's so crystal clear to me.

So, when I drift from that because life is crazy and my environment doesn't support connection, I do know how to come back to myself because I remember.

I remember the feeling of picking up my guitar even though I'm actually terrible at playing. I remember the feeling on an afternoon walk when I reset and feel whole again. I remember the feeling when I stopped doing all the things I "should" and started listening to what works for our family. I remember that feeling when I let go of people or experiences that pained me because they no longer served me.

You will always have an awakening and a remembering of self. When I woke up and realised I was less effective in my role as a mum until I took good care of myself and my needs was the moment I sensed the shift. I had to choose myself again.

Choosing to do something just for yourself each day goes beyond just having snippets of sanity in your daily life, it actually helps to reinforce qualities of strength and resilience, peace and happiness within you.

Do what you love as often as you can manage and listen to your heart's whispers as it guides you back to yourself again. Finding yourself after feeling so lost will be one of the most profound moments you have.

Your authentic self

To be nobody but yourself – in a world which is doing its best, night and day, to make you everybody else –means to fight the hardest battle which any human being can fight; and never stop fighting.

— E.E. CUMMINGS

I've always said that if I could give our children one thing to take forward into their life it would be to know themselves so deeply they won't change for anyone.

There isn't much more empowering than being connected to your authentic self. The one that doesn't change or filter for anyone else.

You came here whole, just like your little ones. Untouched by experiences that all make us question ourselves. The stronger the sense of self we have, the better we handle these moments, the less we feel torn away from our inner self.

This inner self is the ultimate expression of your soul and the essence of who you are. When you began your journey into motherhood she had to change, shifts had to occur to make space. Like I mentioned earlier that change occurs within our souls in order for "mother" to be birthed.

And that doesn't just happen as you physically birth your children, it's a process that happens over and over again throughout motherhood.

Reconnecting with yourself now requires you to remember who you were pre-children, embrace who you became as mother and merge the best qualities of both.

The maiden is the child-free, independent self who is still exploring her own internal landscape of who she really is. In her healthiest expression she is honouring herself, she doesn't change for others or apologise for just being. She stands her ground when needed but is always loving.

As you move out of the maiden stage and into motherhood, this process is called matrescence. The mother is the nurturer, the selfless woman focused on caring for and nourishing her loved ones. She finds an existence of herself outside of her being in her children. In her healthiest expression she is devoted and nurturing of others and also of herself. She doesn't trade her inner self for what is expected of her.

To find yourself again you have to shed all the layers of things that were never you in the first place.

When you are the healthiest expression of maiden or mother...

What does that look like?
What are you doing?
What are your best traits?
Who is surrounding you?

You will have trouble reconnecting with yourself today if you are forever looking into the past and trying to identify yourself with a woman who had a different life, different priorities and a different future ahead of her.

Your expression as a maiden may have included travelling the world, dancing till the sun came up, running marathons, playing in a band or forging a demanding and successful career, most of which needs to be gently set aside in the early days of motherhood, hopefully to be reconnected with when the time is right for you.

But what did you *feel* when you were in these moments? Liberated, free, powerful, centred, proud, creative. Those feelings came from being connected to your inner self, your true self, so that's what we want to tap back into.

You don't have to completely leave the maiden behind to become a mother. In all stages of life there will be parts of you to never be left behind.

I never knew how much I would change internally as a mother. Everything in me became more sensitive. I had love pouring out of me and I was more vulnerable than I have ever felt in my life. But it's the best kind of vulnerable.

A mother's love is indescribable, and I am forever grateful that it has changed me in the way it has.

I want you to consider this question, in this moment right now: who are you? You more than anyone know your idiosyncrasies, quirks, preferences, weaknesses and sheer strengths. If you had to use only a couple of sentences to describe yourself, what would they be?

I'm not asking for the filtered version of what you think is the right thing to say or what makes you likeable, lovable and admirable. I want the real description, the one that truly reflects who you are today.

My sentences would go something like this:

I am loyal to my core. I trust people too much and naively believe everyone has the same good heart that I value. I'm self-conscious and worry too much about what other people think. I'm too hard on myself but am relaxed and forgiving of others. I love with all my heart. I am stubborn and defensive. I am kind, nurturing and caring. I adore being a mother but I need something else as well. I have unmet desires and dreams. I am multi-passionate and creative more than I am action oriented and organised.

As individuals, we need to recognise and cherish our uniqueness and live only in authenticity. We have all been created to be special and unlike anyone else. Nobody thinks, cares and loves in the same way you do. This is why connecting with and learning to love ourselves for all of ourselves is critical.

What I want you to remember is this: not one single soul on this earth is anything like you. Isn't that reason enough to stop wishing and hoping to be something different or more?

You have been given grace and knowledge that can show you ultimate happiness. It's all within you, whether it be your parenting or sharing your art with the world or caring for others as a career or having the ability to make people laugh or being incredibly compassionate or coming up with technological ideas that can make waves or simply being an incredible friend.

No matter what your particular contribution is, this is what makes you special and important, and it is what distinguishes you from everyone else.

Don't dull your unique gifts. Instead, connect with them and celebrate them.

Recognition of self is the most loving form of being witnessed. We often feel the need to be witnessed and seen by others, but can you see yourself for all that you are?

Loving your life

We pulled up in the carpark and I felt more nervous than Harry seemed, but we mothers generally do the worrying thing so well. It was his first time ever attending before-school care.

Harry was now in Grade 1 and was in the Support Unit at a lovely local school. He was going from strength to strength. He was so much more confident, he tried super hard and he was happy. Finally, he was happy.

But despite all this I still worried. Would he cope with the new kids in the morning time slot? Will it set him up for a bad day and poke all his sensory triggers?

We walked in together and as I chatted with the carer, she commented how much he had started to open up on his days with them. My heart filled. Positive feedback about your kids is always the best, but when you have kids with special needs sometimes you have to wait longer for these moments and they mean so much when they come.

As we stood watching, Harry was hanging by the side watching the bigger boys play tag.

I remember when he started school he was frightened by the "big boys" charging through the playground before the bell went.

Now he seemed comfortable, sitting back but smiling.

A gorgeous little human came over, probably four years Harry's senior and said "Hey mate, wanna play tag with us?"

My heart melted. There are still good kids, thank you, God. Harry's entire face lit up; he nodded his head frantically without words then without hesitation raced into the playground.

The smile on his face, and mine, was ear to ear. Tears were streaming down my face... and the carer's too. We both knew how huge that moment was.

We are faced with so many struggles in motherhood that at times having awareness of all the incredible things can feel separate from us. The joy, the things we love, all the moments our hearts were full is why we become parents. For the blessing of *that* love.

Whenever I am having a hard week, I think of this day with Harry. All the moments of struggle, tears and hardship faded away in an instant. That moment makes all my troubles fade away.

Focusing on the love in your life and being positive will help you feel better about the days that are harder. There is goodness there, and if right now you feel so overwhelmed you can't see that just yet, that's okay, Beautiful. You are in survival mode right now; the goodness is still there even if you can't see it just yet.

In the times when the world around you may be casting dark shadows or it seems like the rain will never end, remember the rain does end. It's all too easy for us to hold onto the bad stuff when it comes along, which is why we have to consciously feel the good stuff to remind ourselves it's there.

Tell me about the beauty, your rainbows,
the laughter and the smiles that beam across your face.

Tell me about the fire in your belly, that surging passion,
the place where your dreams live.

Tell me of the souls that are your lifeblood,
their little feet, the giggles, the one who stole your heart.
Tell me how you love, how you want to be loved.

Being a parent is the biggest reality check you will ever get. It's like the fertility gods decided to smack you square between the eyes and say *You'd better hold onto your seat, Sweetheart, because you haven't seen wild until these kids arrive.*

There is no doubt that my world changed for the better when I met my husband and we started a family. It's true that it has been the most challenging of times for us emotionally and financially and for our relationship, but all that hard work is rewarded a thousand times over when it comes to watching our little ones explore their world. It's one of the things I love most about my life as their mama.

More than anything, however, I love that I have soul partners to share my journey with. The five of us are a team and every day I learn and witness something new and magical about our kids and Spooner. It never gets boring and I will love it forever.

I love the bond in my family that is unbreakable and unshakable, no matter how many tantrums, time-outs and meltdowns we all endure. I love that I now appreciate and get excited about the simple things in life, like finding lizards in the backyard, watching planes take off and having the world around me slow down so I can actually see and experience it.

Reconnecting with yourself is asking yourself questions about who you are and what you love. These two questions can tell you everything you need to know about yourself.

Getting in touch with what you love about your life makes it easier for you to live in the present moment and tune into that loving vibe on a daily basis.

I know that for me, consciously taking the time to remind myself of what I love about my life helps make the crazy times as a mama more manageable.

Whenever stuff gets tough and you want to crumble, hide in the bathroom and cry, or just take the easy road, remind yourself of what drives you, moves you, inspires you and nourishes you. Then you can accept your life in the present moment and know that this is just a moment. You will appreciate all that your journey entails, and connect once again with your true self. She knows who she is, what she loves and what she needs to do to fill her soul.

Stop caring what other people think

Caring too much about what other people think and letting their opinions dictate or influence our behaviour and emotions is a dangerous place to be, but it is a place that a lot of us find ourselves in because we believe that acceptance comes to us externally and not from within. We place ownership of ourselves into someone else's hands and essentially ask them if we are okay to be us.

When we fully accept ourselves for who we are and what we believe in, we no longer feel the need to search externally for approval and the only opinion that truly matters is ours and ours alone.

There is a big difference between valuing someone's opinion and idolising or caring about it more than your own.

When you become a parent, everyone from your mother to the owner of the corner store will have an opinion on how you should raise your child. From the moment our babies arrive our mothering skills are being watched.

Midwives check on us from day one, our family wants to help us out or make comments from a distance, women in our mothers' group want to talk for hours on end about what they do and don't do, mums at school compare their children's grades and extracurricular activities, and on and on it goes in what can sometimes feel like a constant cycle of watching, comparing and judging.

Some of this may be unintentional, but if you aren't headstrong in your decisions as a mum (and let's face it, we are never one hundred per cent sure all the time) you will feel some level of pressure. Other people's opinions can begin to hold more value. If there is a space within you where your self-belief isn't as solid as it could be, then in will creep the need to get approval from others.

When we care about what another person thinks we are seeking their approval. Remember, we all just want to be loved.

Women get caught up in comparison and worrying about what other people think because we handed the power over to that archetype mother. We decided that story we talked about before is true. That we don't know ourselves better than anyone else. That we "should" be a certain way.

When that doubt crept in, we started seeking external validation. We cared way too much about what everyone else thinks because we lost our own connection with ourselves.

As women and as mothers, we need to get more tenacious about what we believe in because we cannot heal and change ourselves if we don't let go of those external opinions.

Trust me when I say I know what I'm talking about here. I care way too much about other people's opinions. My low self-worth feeds the idea in my head that in order to feel better I need external approval and acceptance and the way to get that is through caring about what people think.

I recently saw an interview with an inspiring woman who had been diagnosed with terminal cancer. She is a young mother of four beautiful children, the youngest of who has Down syndrome.

She, like all mothers, had dedicated her entire world to being a mum. When she received her diagnosis, a light bulb went off and she realised that life is too short to care what anybody thinks.

She went out and got herself a platinum blonde pixie haircut along with some rocking tattoos she had always wanted. She was sick of fitting into the box of who and what she thought she needed to be. The woman she felt herself to be inside was not being represented on the outside because she put too much emphasis on what other people thought of her.

We don't actually need a life-changing moment to stop caring what other people think, whether it is about our hairdo, our parenting skills, our role as a daughter-in-law or anything at all. We just need to care more about what we think – not everyone else. Trade their opinion for your own.

Are you going to let other people's opinions shape who you are or are you ready to step up and be the creator of your own life? Any life that is dictated by someone other than yourself is not your life.

Stop worrying about being a perfect mother and what all the other mums are doing. Do what feels good for you. People will always have their own opinions, people will always judge, and women, well, some may always be bitches.

Now I definitely don't like talking down about women, I'm all about empowering. But there are plenty of women who do externalise their pain and tear women down instead of building them up.

We can't change humans and how we behave but we can change whether we place more importance on ourselves or someone else.

The more work I do on myself, the countless mentors I listen to and the books I read all come back to the same thing. Other people's opinions of you are a reflection upon them, not you.

In other words, it is more about those people having some underlying issue within themselves that they feel the need to project onto you. If you can see it that way, then you will understand that their opinion isn't really about you at all and you can stop caring about it.

Every time I have been caught in a spiral of worrying about what other people think of me, I reflect back. I look at the situation and bring it back to me. Why do I feel the need to care about or want to influence this person's opinion of me? Why am I triggered by that person's words or actions?

There is always a lesson. There is always another way you can turn within.

Living your life being dictated by others' opinions, whether they accept you or not or whether you think you're good enough compared to them, is a painful life. It takes up brain space. We need our brain space; my goodness do mothers need all the available brain space they have.

Use your energy wisely, if you can clear another barrier to you living closer to your truest self then do so. It's your life, remember? No one else's.

The importance of self-care

When the well is dry, we know the worth of water.
— BENJAMIN FRANKLIN

When our well is empty no one can be nourished. Not one member of your family benefits from you being depleted, exhausted and broken.

We think we are serving our family when we keep pushing on but they are getting half of us, maybe less. And when you try to pour from an empty cup it is futile.

Tired and worn-out women need to be nourished and taken care of yet the world we live in encourages us to keep on keeping on. We don't admit "defeat", we don't take breaks and we definitely don't put ourselves first. This results in our tiredness turning to depletion and breaking point. We can only do so much after all.

Too many of us mothers are waiting until we are broken to make changes. Too many partners, family and friends assume everything is alright and don't ask the questions that need to be asked sooner. We need their awareness and our own.

Everything we have been talking about comes back to the idea of self-care, which is really about acknowledging who you are and nourishing your existence exactly as it is. It means making sure you are living the strongest, brightest, most beautiful version of yourself and not the filtered, restricted, more "acceptable" one.

The catch here is that in order to reconnect and truly love and care for yourself, you must nourish your mind, body and soul.

Without giving yourself the love and care you need to survive, your sense of acceptance and gratitude for who you are becomes darkened by exhaustion and feelings of being overwhelmed or always needing more.

Self-care is...

- Getting a massage
- Going for a quiet walk
- Time with girlfriends
- Buying an outfit that makes you feel good
- Lighting a candle
- Taking a bath
- Reading a book
- Hitting a spin class

Self-care is also...

- Saying no without guilt
- Asking for the help you need
- Forgiving yourself for all your perceived faults
- Not comparing yourself to others
- Letting go of relationships and situations that feel toxic
- Accepting your humanness
- Honouring your deepest desires
- Setting clear boundaries

The second list is actually more important than the first, but the first list of small incidentals actually makes the second list of self-care easier to achieve.

Small moments are what motherhood is all about and we can try with almighty strength to change our lives overnight but it really is about small and achievable steps.

Little by little we need to make a conscious decision to choose ourselves, to honour ourselves and to prioritise how we care for ourselves.

I deserve to be cared for as much as others.
It is not selfish to take care of myself, in doing so
I am able to fully care for others.

We need to understand that we can't possibly enact change and bring happiness into our lives if we don't take responsibility for our own physical and emotional wellbeing. It's vitally important that you learn to accept and believe that you are worthy of love, attention and nurturing as well.

Your role as a mother does not mean you should give up your own entitlement to being loved and cared for. Just because you are a nurturer does not mean that you should be deprived of being nurtured in turn.

Most of us have such an innate mothering instinct that of course the priorities and needs of our children and family come first, but this shouldn't be at our own expense. In fact, looking after ourselves is paramount to the success of a happy family.

It's like the daggy saying that Spooner always whips out: "Happy wife, happy life." I know he has a whole other meaning to this phrase and as funny, yet also annoying, as that can be, it's also true.

If the wife, mother, carer and nurturer in the home isn't happy, then who else can be? Our own happiness affects the mood and wellbeing of our loved ones which is why self-care is imperative for all mamas.

Self-care is about taking the time to nurture and maintain our bodies, minds and souls. Without giving these the attention they need you are bound to end up with an empty cup. Self-care has to become part of your routine.

Ten minutes a day

I was told by several people when I first was diagnosed with postnatal depression that I needed to try to allocate ten minutes a day to any activity that was for me and me alone. *So much easier said than done* I thought instantly. *When on earth am I going to find ten minutes?*

Ten minutes isn't much time to find but when you're a burnt-out mum running on caffeine and adrenalin it feels like just another thing to add to the ever-growing list. Our time as mums feels so elusive and precious that seizing just ten minutes of it for ourselves seems like a massive ask.

Here's how I thought about it to make finding those ten free minutes much more achievable. In your average day you will have about fourteen hours when you're awake. Within those fourteen waking hours, there are *eighty-four* ten-minute slots of time.

When I broke it down like that instead of getting caught up in the idea that I simply had no spare time whatsoever, I realised that it was possible for me to find those ten minutes and give them to myself as a gift.

I encourage you to choose just one of those eighty-four ten-minute slots that are available to you each day and spend it doing an activity that restores and inspires you.

One day a week

This one day per week might be for a fitness class, an art class, dinner with girlfriends, a self-care full moon ritual, a long bath with wine in hand… something you have been promising yourself for months on end. These are the ones that we put in the too-hard basket and end up slumped on the lounge exhausted with no desire to do much else.

Pick a day that works, when you know your partner is home or someone else can watch the kids, you need to make it fail-safe. Commit to being there for yourself every week, whether it's the same activity or just every Wednesday night for example.

Don't feel bad for walking out the door, even if the kids are being crazy that day and begging you stay. This is your one day of the week when you get an hour or so to yourself, so don't miss the opportunity to enjoy it through feeling guilty.

If you find it difficult to commit week in and week out, try inviting a friend along to help keep you motivated and accountable or explain to your partner how imperative this time is for you to take care of your mental wellbeing.

It has to be non-negotiable, and you need to commit to yourself.

One day a month
This is a day when the kids are in care or at school, or you get the grandparents to pop over and help out for the day.

We all have days like that here and there, but this one is special.

No matter how convenient it may be for you to shop for groceries without the kids or pay the bills and run errands, on this one day per month I would like you to do something that is solely for you.

Come home from school drop-off and go back to bed for a few hours. Laze on the lounge and watch a movie or get a massage and meet a friend for lunch, flog yourself at boxing class or OM your way to yoga bliss.

Whatever you choose to do, make sure it nourishes you.

At the end of the day, there is no doubt you will feel incredibly refreshed. The guilt stays at the door, ignore everything else that needs to be done that isn't life threatening (no, a laundry full of washing does not qualify) and switch off to the outside and on to yourself.

Over the years I have been stuck in a period where my physical health has not been great, in fact, it's been terrible. I was over-stressed, pushing myself to my limits, saying no to myself all the time and suffering along the way.

I caught myself one day wound up and so cross at the kids, I screamed at them "Why aren't you listening to me!"

A pretty standard question (a.k.a. outburst) for any mother. But the moment those words came out I suddenly realised I wasn't talking to them. I was talking to myself.

I had been having an issue with the kids not listening to me for what felt like months and it was the latest thing that was grinding me. Yelling at them and asking about their ignorance was a regular thing. So was pushing myself aside and not prioritising my needs.

It dawned on me that it was not cranky mummy speaking, but my inner knowing. My soul inside was begging me to pay attention.

Why aren't you listening to me? Why aren't you taking care of yourself? Your health is suffering, listen to your body, please.

That realisation changed everything for me.

My body was sending me signs that something needed to change. The yelling at the kids, the anger, the resentment, the physical ailments – my body was showing me all the red flags but I just kept on going.

I'm far from perfect now but I can see I let myself get way too far down the slope with my self-care. I had switched off my own awareness so much that struggling and not thriving had become a normal and acceptable state for me to be in. I had let go of self-care and started believing that sacrificing myself for everyone else in my family was just accepted and expected. I was not doing anything much for myself and had cemented the idea in my head that the only value I had to anyone was as a mum.

Eventually, my physical body was so broken and uncared for and my mental wellbeing had become so unravelled that my world crumbled around me.

I know we can press pause on this spiral of women falling apart. To do so, first you have to believe one very important thing… **you deserve to be loved and nurtured as well.**

Re-loving

I wonder how many days in my life I have wasted thinking about my body and how it doesn't live up to my expectations. How many hours I have spent changing outfits only to change them again and again? How many minutes have I spent overanalysing the dark circles under my eyes, my saggy and wrinkled belly, my lumps and bumps and whatever else is going on back there? More than I would care to know, I'm sure. Covering up my body in searing heat all because I feel like this body isn't good enough. What a waste! I've felt like this about myself for longer than I can remember and I am so tired of it. I don't even know if what I see is true anymore. I know my image of myself is warped I just don't honestly know how to stop doing that. I desperately want to look in the mirror and love who I see, accept who I see. I notice how quickly Jacob picks up on the things we say and do. Does he see this too? Does he hear Mummy constantly asking Daddy "How do I look?" Does he see me look in disgust at myself in the mirror? Am I surrounding my kids with negative body images? Will they expect too much of their

partners and want them to be physically 'perfect'? Will they judge
their own bodies as harshly as I do? Am I inadvertently raising
unconscious and judgemental children? I have a choice to break this
cycle, if not only for me, then also for my kids. From today on, and
on any other day I may falter, I will affirm that my body is worth
loving – every single square inch of her. Even when I don't feel like
saying it, I'm going to tell her she is beautiful, she is imperfectly
perfect and that I love her. I love all of me, I must.

Finding yourself again is one thing, loving yourself again is a whole other ball game. It's asking us to smash down any barriers to love that stand in our way. It's welcoming all parts of yourself in an open embrace and being willing to accept yourself wholly as you are.

It's also banishing every concept and idea of what the "perfect" woman is like. Everything from how she looks, what she wears, how she feels and what she says.

Re-loving is starting again. We lost ourselves in motherhood and as we are finding ourselves again, we have to reconnect with the entirety of ourselves. We need to begin again and foster deep, unrelenting self-love, to right the wrongs, to make new patterns and move forward with a new mindset.

Motherhood may have shocked you to your core, but it also made you greater than ever before:

Motherhood changes us deep on a cellular level, you will never be the same after birthing a child into this world. Never. And thank God for that. This is when we step into ownership of our truest self, when we embody the divinity in us that we have been journeying towards our whole lives.

Motherhood is a culmination of all the moments before, it will be the greatest mirror to reflect on all the times we have been and are forgetting our own truth.

Nothing will break you down and help you be reborn like motherhood does. This is your moment to be willing to burn down all the old stories you have told yourself so you can be reborn again from the ashes.

This is your opportunity to leave shame and guilt at the door and welcome full acceptance of yourself.

Your wounded inner self

Each of us had a unique upbringing. Each of us was once an innocent child, impressionable and soaking in all our surroundings.

From a very young age we watched the role of woman and man, mother and father being played out before our eyes, we created our own stories about what women and mothers look like.

We all had experiences in childhood, our teenage years and adulthood that challenged our inner knowing and pushed us further away from who we were meant to be.

As women we have lived a much different path than men. Throughout history women have been stripped of their power and fed the acceptable version of beauty. We are now not only righting the wrongs from our own personal experiences but challenging and taking back ownership of women's potential.

Every relationship, every moment all came together to make you who you are. The good and the bad has all shaped your opinions, expectations and perceptions of the world.

We all have that part in ourselves that is longing to be loved, this is your inner self, inner child, divinity, whatever term you want to give it. That is the part of you that has been wounded from your experiences and every time you choose a fear-based response you are acting from the space of that wounded inner self.

Whenever someone denied you the love you were seeking you stored that away, you held it within.

Every experience, including the small everyday stuff, will shape us.

We listen to the ego voice in our head that tells us we are not worthy because we are not slim enough, not sporty enough, not curvy enough, not successful enough, not rich enough, not happy enough, not strong enough, not wild enough, not relaxed enough.

Yet there is always truth; our wounds are not our truth, *they lead us to our truth*.

Is your truth there if you are able to look in the mirror and love the woman you see with all her curves and bumps, her tired eyes and dry, thinning hair? What about when you're able to appreciate the smarts, spirit and quirky personality that lies beneath the surface?

However you define it, self-love is your key to inviting grace into your life. This is where it's at. When you love yourself everything else really does fall into place.

Healing the wounds of your inner self and reshaping your experience of love towards yourself requires you to welcome acknowledgement, acceptance and appreciation.

Don't worry, I get it, re-loving yourself after you have children is no mean feat. It's tough and it can be confronting. Over time I had been shrinking and hiding parts of myself hoping no one else would notice all the faults and flaws in my being. Denying who you are is a painful process.

I don't know about you, but I am up for the challenge. I am so sick of not loving the body I see in the mirror, of always picking on it and hoping something will change. I am no longer willing to listen to the belittling voice in my head that tells me my personality needs some alteration in order for me to be liked or accepted. My spirit will not be dulled anymore.

If we can acknowledge the wounds as they are, knowing we can't change our past experiences or reject our feelings forever, just by witnessing them alone we allow space for our souls to feel lighter.

You don't have to do deep trauma work – and in some cases, we may never be ready to address trauma – but just see and witness any experiences that have caused you pain.

Acceptance comes when we understand that we cannot change the past hurts we have experienced and we know that moving on does not mean forgetting or forgiveness, but it does mean letting go. When we let go of something it no longer has a hold on us.

We often don't realise how much a painful experience consumes our lives, we have trouble letting it go because we need that pain justified and explained. Acceptance doesn't mean you're okay with the pain, but it does mean you want to let it go.

Appreciation follows when you have worked through the first stages. You can see the lessons. You're grateful for the toxic relationship that now reminds you of your own worth and how you deserve to be treated. You're grateful for your family's differences because it reminds you how important it is to stay true to who you are. You're grateful for the depression and anxiety because it made you see everything inside that no longer worked and find yourself again.

Part of healing our wounded inner self means peeling back the layers on the ways we break ourselves down and how we self-sabotage, even if we don't realise we are.

Self-sabotage

Have you ever had the experience of being offered an incredible opportunity but something within you questions whether or not you deserve it? What about when you really want a new outfit for an event, but you feel guilty about spending the money or berate yourself for looking like a plumpy hot mess? How about just being able to accept a compliment with dignity instead of dismissing the well-intended words as something the person didn't mean?

Such moments of acceptance and appreciation come our way each and every day but so often we find a way to disregard them. We just love to be our own self-saboteur, and most of the time we don't even realise we are doing it.

Why do women self-sabotage?
Is it partly because we enjoy being the victim?
Is it easier for us to blend into the background and not shine too brightly?
Are we more comfortable with being mediocre?
Are we too scared to be our very best?

We want so deeply to be loved and accepted as we are, but our fear of judgement and of not being accepted drives us away from being who we truly are.

This can be true for everyone, but when it comes to self-sabotage women really can take the cake and show men how it's done.

Most men seem to have the ability to really just accept themselves as they are and not care what anyone else thinks about them. That's not to say that they don't have their insecurities, but the majority of men don't spend hours in front of the mirror analysing and picking apart their bodies.

It's because men didn't grow up being shown and told what their bodies should look like in the same toxic ways as women. They weren't conditioned to believe that Barbie was the image of perfection and an obedient housewife was the gold standard of achievement for women. We have a lot to undo.

The same kind of problem arises when it comes to loving our souls. Countless times I have had dreams that feel so big and inspiring, hobbies that would light me up, life changes that could fulfil me deeply, but I let them all go for fear of not being good enough. This fear was driven by my ego telling me that my ideas weren't valued, that I wasn't allowed to stand out, and who did I think I was to be chasing that dream anyway?

Sometimes it just seems easier to side with the ego – because, after all, it's been blaring in stereo in our minds throughout our whole life –while our inner guide speaks in whispers and simply hopes we can hear her through any pause in the noise.

It's easy to stick with the stories, they become comfortable after a while. Then one day out of nowhere we almost feel like we may explode if we have to stay inside that box for one more day.

Remember, the path of least resistance is not always the best one to take. What if you could choose instead to lead your life by loving and accepting your body and soul just as they are? What if you chose to halt the self-sabotage in its tracks?

I promise to love myself just as I am.
I am deserving of good things.
I deeply love and accept myself.

We don't mean to self-sabotage, we just don't know any better. It's like we have been kept in these neat and tidy boxes. Following the rules, not making waves, being comfortable, fitting in, being the way we were always told to be.

But this is a learned behaviour and any learned behaviour can be unlearned.

We need to understand it actually isn't our fault but a history that didn't know better and didn't honour us. Women now know the difference but we still have work to do to unlearn all those behaviours and perceptions we picked up along the way.

Understanding that we self-sabotage due to our sense of not being good enough or worthy is the beginning of unlearning a lifetime of imbalance. It is not fitting into a box, in fact, it's not fitting into anything at all.

Inadequacy

A million times over, the theme that rings true in any woman's life when things are not in alignment is that she is caught in the feeling of *not being good enough*. Not good enough at being a mum, not good enough to chase that promotion, not good enough to start a new home-based business, not good enough to stick to an exercise plan, not good enough to fit in with the new mothers' group, not good enough to feel sexy in those jeans on date night, not good enough to be who she is, just as she is.

I'm not sure what bar we are supposed to be measuring up to here, but it seems that we all feel we fall short of it.

This feeling that you can't be at peace with yourself as you are has to be the most painful struggle your soul can bear. Countless times I have hidden away in the bathroom and cried for help, cried about my imperfections and cried over how this parenting gig is just so hard. I've cried that I'm not cut out for this job and cried even more at the loss of the idealistic dream of being a mum that I had so longed for.

I'm sure many more tears will flow, just as I am sure I will ultimately lose my life to an injury sustained by standing on LEGO. But somewhere deep beneath those tears, beneath the noise and mental chatter, my inner voice is still there telling me that I am good enough.

This feeling of not being good enough is inherently behind all of the emotions and excuses we use to hold us back, to stop us reaching for more. It is what won't allow us to be our authentic selves.

This inadequacy has been programmed into us from an experience in life where somewhere along the line we felt we didn't measure up. We could never please our parents, we never felt successful in our careers, we had many failed relationships... any perceived "failure" in life we use to reinforce this idea of being inadequate, of not being good enough.

Inspiring life coach Anthony Robbins said "Our beliefs about what we are and what we can be precisely determine what we can be." So essentially when we believe that we aren't enough, we will never be enough. We will always place limitations on our own potential and run in this vicious cycle.

How then do we silence the persistent voice that tells us we are not good enough and make more space for believing that we *are* enough?

As I have mentioned, our ego or inner mean girl can only thrive when we become the victim and let it control our thoughts and behaviour. The answer is to take the power away from your ego.

Start by acknowledging your own inner knowing and begin to listen to those around you when they compliment you. Embrace the kindness offered in those words and really believe what you hear.

There is a bit of a balancing act here between your internal and external worlds. We can't often hear or see our own truth, but others can. It's the gift of connection and what humans can bring to each other in a relationship.

Usually, we are much harsher judges of ourselves than we are of others, so turning to our external world and the comments of those who love us is a good way to start breaking down our internal judgement and feelings of inadequacy.

And remember the *I am Worthy* list we created back in Part I? You can use that list here too.

Keep in mind that inadequacy is an internally created emotion. No one can force you to feel it. Other people can contribute but it's your responsibility to shift this story.

You are not inadequate. None of us are. We are different and unique. That does not mean we are inadequate and have shortcomings that we should feel conscious of. It means we are all so beautifully unique that it should be celebrated.

Comparison

I remember once heading down with our family and my younger brother to a cool beach on the North Shore in Sydney. On the way there, I wasn't overly concerned about my body. In fact, I'd been feeling great about it after making a conscious effort to not only eat well and exercise as often as I could, but also to invite acceptance and self-love back into my life.

I'd had a gutful of feeling bad about myself and was on the I-love-my-body train and enjoying the ride.

Until that is, I set foot on this beach.

Mums with rocking bodies were everywhere, hot bikinis, cool beach bags and just looking like everything I all of a sudden didn't feel like.

My first thought was to retreat into my towel and keep all of me well and truly covered. All the work I had been doing on learning to re-love my body momentarily went out the window, because in that one instant I compared myself to a bunch of women I didn't even know.

And that's the point. *I knew nothing about them.* Not their lifestyle, not their health, not their family situation – nothing. I was comparing their highlight reel to all the years of my own self-love journey. The two are never the same.

What I realised upon reflection – and mind you, this did not happen until I was in the car on the way home, because up until then I was a paranoid mess inside my own head – is that making comparisons with no background information is like looking at the cover of a book with no pages.

I could see on the outside what these women appeared to be in my eyes, but in reality, I could understand nothing of their story. They could have an incredible genetic lineage (and don't let anyone tell you this is a cop-out because some people are just born with top pick from the blessed gene pool), they could work incredibly hard every day of the week to achieve that body, they may have a husband who is home to help with the kids, they could have an incredibly supportive family and a team of babysitters, or they may just be an incredible mum who balances it all and can rock out a bikini body that is admirable for anyone, let alone a mother of three.

And who am I to take any of that away from them?

They could also be unhappy inside. Despite how I perceived them, they could also be battling their own inner demons about their bodies. Finding a woman without body shaming issues of some kind is like finding the match for all those missing socks in your laundry. We *all* have our own body love stories.

All I saw were bodies and it triggered every moment of body shame in me. Worse still, while I was in comparison mode and putting myself down they were enjoying their beach day. Most of them despite what may have been playing in their minds, were still playing in their swimmers with their kids.

On the car ride home I was more upset that I wasted a fun day out while the background story in my head was a complete distraction from all the good things that were happening.

Comparing yourself to the external image you see of other women and families will only hold you back on your own path to growth. It is nothing more than a way of laying shame on yourself.

By comparing yourself with other women, you are saying to yourself that what she has, does, looks like or says is better or more than what you can offer – and it's just not true.

Let me tell you something powerful I have learnt over the past couple of years. No matter how awesome I thought everyone else was, and how un-awesome I tagged myself to be – *my moment was coming.* That moment when I realised, felt and knew deep in my core I should never try to be anything more than myself.

That moment is there waiting for all of us.

I just had to be patient. I had to work through some of my junk. I had to step into the shadows and make decisions to choose love instead of fear and then grow. I had to allow myself to be vulnerable so acceptance could introduce itself to me.

From a young age we measure ourselves against our peers and compete with them for approval. We are constantly surrounded and moulded by comparison with idealised and unrealistic versions of the people we are supposed to aspire to be like. You have to look this way, do this to be successful, play this sport, own this phone and do this and this and this.

It all comes back to being okay with ourselves as we are and living in our authenticity. We are all weird and quirky in all the right kinda ways. There isn't a "one way" and when we realise that we really don't need to compare.

Shame

Deep and thick in amongst the mess of not being good enough and mum guilt is shame. It's a self-imposed tightness and judgement that we place upon ourselves. We believe we are so wrong about our decisions, our thoughts or what we have done, to the point that we persecute ourselves.

Shame has enough strength behind it to do serious damage, because this is the never-spoken-about emotion. The heaviness of that feeling is too large for us to share so we store it deep down within. Any emotion that is stored within us like that can't be good for our overall emotional and physical health.

In the early days after my postnatal depression and anxiety diagnosis I lived in shame. I just didn't know how to get out of it. It was the deepest and darkest of holes.

Saying I felt sick to my stomach with shame and desperation wouldn't even come close to describing it. All those feelings of inadequacy about being a useless mother, all my fears about everyone else's judgement over my failure, all my disappointment that I couldn't be the wife and mother my husband needed me to be, and all my hopelessness over the fact I felt I was letting my darling children down… it all came raining down on me, hard.

Shame is the stage after guilt, it's when we feel guilty for doing or feeling a certain way then deciding to stuff that guilt inside and never share it again.

I still have moments when it creeps in and whispers in my ear *Remember the time you stopped breastfeeding early?* or *Remember how you put so much strain on your husband with your emotional demands during your depression?* And *Oh and remember that time when you snapped and screamed uncontrollably at your toddler after he had meltdown after meltdown?*

Over time as I become stronger within myself the shame has less to grab onto. I worry less about my "mistakes" and love myself regardless of the bad days and when I'm in that headspace shame has no place. The shameful thoughts are still there, only now I do not buy into them.

Shame thrived while I was at my lowest and most vulnerable. It was one of the things keeping me in that vulnerable inactive state.

When we feel we have failed at being a mother that can strike us like a sword to the heart. Placing shame on motherhood is painful. We can shift this mindset by becoming better at practising self-forgiveness, detaching from the expectations and embracing what is.

Embracing your birthing story

As I sat there holding our last-born, Ruby, in my arms, I felt the greatest sense of achievement. In fact, I felt invincible.

This feeling was new for me. I had never had this sense of pride or achievement for any of my previous births.

Ruby's birth had gone just as I had hoped. I felt connected to my body, I was listening to myself before anyone else, I had no intervention and it all felt beautiful.

I remember crying with relief that I had finally achieved the birth I truly hoped for from the start. That relief was tinged with sadness on what I felt I had missed out on with the boys.

Jacob's birth was long, arduous and stressful. His heart rate was elevated so they recommended an induction. When it's your first baby and the nurses look concerned, you do as they say. I didn't understand that an induction reduces your chances of delivering without intervention as you lose the natural progressive stages of labour.

I was labelled a "failure to progress" and after ten hours and only two-centimetre dilation I was offered an epidural. I was exhausted and terrified, but I took the doctor's advice. At that point I felt I had failed our baby, myself and Spooner.

After Jacob's long-anticipated arrival, I lost consciousness in the shower, losing large amounts of blood. Jacob's first few hours were spent snuggled on Daddy's chest because Mummy was shattered, both physically and emotionally.

Twenty months later I was feeling anxious and panicked in the lead up to Harry's birth. I didn't know it at the time, but I had severe depression and anxiety, which I just put down to hormones, no sleep and environmental factors.

I was beyond petrified of having a birth experience like we did for Jacob. Add into that my anxiety and I was a wreck.

Harry was ten days overdue and it was recommended again I have an induction. As soon as I felt those labour pains ramp up, I almost felt like it was impossible to deliver this baby. The fear that rose in me was so intense. I chose to have an epidural purely from the fear I had about reliving our first birth.

Harry's arrival into the world felt uneventful in some ways, I felt disconnected from him. I certainly didn't feel like a priority in the hospital. We were left for long periods without checks despite asking for them. So many aspects of his birth felt like I wasn't supported or honoured in any way. I became a number in a bed not a woman bringing life into this world.

All three of my birthing stories were completely different. Each one of them unique. The common thread for the boys, after doing some inner work on this over the years, was that I didn't believe in my inner power. I was disconnected from the belief that I was strong enough emotionally and physically to do this. During Ruby's birth I had to face this fear that birthing was something I was not good at and had failed in the past. Each of them was so different yet they all taught me something – my unconditional love for them was far greater and expansive than my beliefs about our birthing stories.

I wanted to share my birth experiences with you because I know this is a deep wound for many of us. We may not have the birthing experience we had hoped for and then often, we aren't given the space to be able to talk about it afterwards. No one else feels the same enormity of what just happened to you physically, emotionally and spiritually.

Heartbreakingly for many mothers, their birthing and pregnancy stories are of loss and devastation. Not only do we deal with the grief of that loss but also the guilt and shock that can come with a miscarriage, stillbirth or early loss of your child.

Right now, I want to honour you, all of you. I want to witness you for all of your strength, triumph, disappointment, fear and guilt. Please know that know that no matter how you feel about your birthing experience it is all valid. I'm not going to let you sweep any of this under the carpet, because birth is far too magnificent for it not to be witnessed.

I hope that you are one of many women who was able to have a birth that felt nourishing, connected and empowering. Yet, if you are one of many, many mothers who had a birth that felt frightening, disappointing and like you were not in control, then I see you.

If you are a mother who lost her baby and feels the deepest heartache, injustice or guilt then I see you. You are entitled to feel any and all of the raw emotions that comes with this loss and I wish there were more words to describe the profound way in which I want to honour you and your story.

Birthing shame and trauma is a very concerning aspect of birth in modern society. Too many mothers come out the other side of their birth experience feeling like they have failed, like they didn't do it the "right way" or that they have let down themselves, their child and families.

Part of this stems from a system that for too many years has moved away from an honouring of the female body and towards a disconnection of women from their intuition. We hand our power and decision making over to our medical team because that's what we are told is the way it's done. We trust in medicine. But many of us we have lost the internal belief that we are able to do this. We have lost our own trust in ourselves. We have forgotten that if we listen within we do have the wisdom to do what our body needs, to feel into the process of birth and when we have reached our limits.

Medical labels like "failure to progress" and "maternal exhaustion" for me feel like red flags that women are being categorised not honoured.

Are we connected into our bodies enough to flow with the birth, therefore supporting our progression through the stages? Are we supported, nurtured and emotionally encouraged so that we can move through contractions with more ease and not have long ordeals that lead to complete exhaustion?

I am in full support of the midwives and doctors who support women and children through birth and if and when medical intervention is required, there is no denying this. I had some wonderful midwives supporting me through my births, they gave me space when required and reminded me of my own desires for the birth.

But there are also times when we don't feel grounded in what we want and connected to our own wisdom we lose faith in ourselves. When the birthing process ramps up, when there are complications without faith we look to everyone outside of ourselves.

I wonder if women were more aware of the spectrum of experiences in birthing and were connected to the inner knowing, how many births would be smoother and how many of us may come out the other side much more positive and not feeling like we failed.

Doulas and birthing support nurses have become so prevalent in our society, which I find so refreshingly beautiful. They have answered the call of many women who knew they needed a different kind of support.

Again, the same message seems to be so crystal clear – it's not the mothers failing themselves or their children, it is the patriarchal system and society's expectations that are failing us.

Are we really being properly prepared for birth? Are ante-natal classes, family and friends covering everything or are they leaving out some crucial information. Birth is natural, unpredictable and how you feel during and after the process is just as natural and unpredictable.

I know healing hearts broken from birth experiences is a long process and time does tend to these wounds in some ways. Talking about it openly and honestly does help; not feeling as though you need to hide your experience and just being free to express your unique experience.

Too often I hear women talk about their birth/s and follow it with an explanation. It's like we feel the need to justify why it wasn't "perfect" or why we felt it was.

Decisions about inductions, pain relief, vaginal or non-vaginal births, extractions and episiotomies are moments in time. They may have been a decision you made with your inner knowing, or one you made reluctantly. Either way, you are allowed to talk about it freely and feel those deep emotions. You are allowed to tell your story without fear of judgement.

How do we move forward and embrace our birthing stories? We welcome acceptance and we forgive ourselves. We accept that how it eventuated was how it was meant to be, no matter how much that may pain us.

When we are able to welcome acceptance in, we move out of the space of trying to change a moment that cannot be changed. Then we forgive ourselves for all we believe we failed at. We welcome the knowledge that we did our very best and that the stories we tell ourselves are not our truth.

Then we remind ourselves that our love for our children is a far greater service to them than that moment of their birth into this world. How we choose to love them for the rest of our lives, whether they are by our sides or in the stars, is more defining a moment for us as mothers than how we birthed them.

I truly hope that one day women can stop labelling complicated births that required intervention or deviated from the desired plans as failures. I truly hope mothers that have lost their babies will know we may never understand why, but that it is of no fault of their own. I truly hope that we can see that our worthiness and greatness as mothers is measured by all the things we do and the intention we do them with.

Weight does not equate to worth

And I said to my body. Softly. 'I want to be your friend.'
It took a long breath. And replied 'I have been waiting my whole life for
this.'
— NAYYIRAH WAHEED

I have a vivid memory from my childhood of being at a Christmas party for my dad's work colleagues. It was a pool party, as they usually are in the hot Australian Christmas season, and the pool was overcrowded with a throng of excitable kids.

I was always that child sitting on the sidelines, nervous about getting involved, always worrying over something and ultimately missing out.

This particular memory stands out to me because I was so self-conscious about my body. I remember sitting on the step of the pool in my pink and purple striped speedos and being paranoid that one of the boys would see the teeny hole I had in my swimming costume, and that I had very small boobs.

As I sat there on the steps of the pool, it was like I was in an alternative reality. All around me, children were flinging themselves into the water, screaming, laughing, not having a worry in the world, and here I was, on my own, worrying about my body to the point that I just sat back and avoided everyone.

This memory scars me to this day, because after discussing it with my dad, I realised that the child on that pool step was only eight years old. She was an innocent young girl who should have been living in the moment and turning roly polys (my favourite thing to do in the pool). Instead, I was living in a world of worry way beyond my years.

Where these heavy and unwarranted concerns in such a young girl came from, I still do not know, but thinking about it breaks my heart. I would be shattered to learn that any of my children had those same feelings of self-consciousness, shame and inadequacy, as I'm sure you would too.

Women's relationships with their bodies and food are complex. Beyond complex.

We've been raised in a patriarchal world, a world perfectly designed for men and not so friendly for us women. The female body has been objectified, sexualised and categorised instead of being revered.

Ancient cultures honoured the female body in all her forms. She was considered beautiful and sacred no matter what her shape was. Menstruation and birth were deeply spiritual and respected.

Over time, the masculine view and influence over the world changed this perception. Women started believing that they can be judged and shamed for their bodies instead of being in awe of their own beauty.

I'm so thankful and inspired watching the rise of the feminine right now. Women changing perceptions, talking about our bodies, our cycles, birth and our sexuality like it is ours to own and not someone else's to dictate – because it is.

I'm not sure I know any women who don't have or haven't battled through some issues surrounding their appearance or weight. It's deep and murky territory and to cut through the bullshit I'm going to start by telling you a few hard truths.

- Your weight is irrelevant to the quality of human being you are.
- Losing weight, gaining muscle and curves won't make you internally happy.

- Women of every possible shape and size *all* have body and confidence issues.
- What you put into your body isn't just about the right foods but the right energy.
- The way you speak to yourself about your body can have a direct influence on how you look.

Let me just repeat that last one. **The way in which you speak to yourself about your body can have a direct influence on how your body looks.** Your words and your attitude towards yourself can shape your physical appearance.

You know what I find more exhausting than sleepless nights with a teething child and hours of toddler whinging with no breaks? It is the constant self-judgement I have held for myself.

It has been an exhausting path looking at myself in the mirror every day and being unhappy and critical about what I see. It's exhausting to be always overanalysing the things I do and don't do, and always wishing I could be better. It is exhausting not feeling good enough and I am tired of it. So tired.

When we want something to change so badly, we can't always accept it as it is. You may feel that accepting your body and appearance isn't something you are capable of. You want to change; you want to feel better about yourself and acceptance won't change anything.

However, acceptance is your gateway. When you can love and accept yourself so deeply internally there will be an external reflection.

People who are stressed and run-down don't generally look like the picture of health. Their shoulders are slumped, their eyes are dark and tired, their smile can be faded. If you spend all your time berating yourself, analysing your body parts, and focusing on your limitations then you will have those feelings reflected physically.

During my pregnancies I definitely had moments of wondering what on earth was going on with this unusually shaped form I saw before me, but most of the time I could embrace my bump and all the bits that came with it. Not until after I had my first son, Jacob, did I understand the physical and emotional challenges I would have to face.

Without a belly to hide behind (well, not a pregnant one at least), I suddenly felt incredibly self-conscious about my weight. I'm sure this is true for most of us. These new bodies of ours, well, they take some time to adjust to. Our bubs don't just pop out and then everything springs back into place – and if you're a mum to more than one child, you'll find each time another one pops out there's even less springing that happens!

There is a big drive in society these days about bouncing back from pregnancy and childbirth. Five-week celebrity transformations get splashed all over magazines and social media. All of this just puts more emphasis on those ideas of being it all, having it all and living up to some impossible ideal – which means very little attention gets given to allowing your body to rest, recover and rejuvenate in its own good time.

Now, I'm not saying you should sit around on your beautiful, plump new booty and do nothing until, say, the kids go to school, because I do believe movement and being healthy is crucial for our physical health and even more so for our mental health. What I am saying is to do that fabulous physical exercise for the *right reasons* and at the *right time*. Make sure your motivation to move is about feeling better, getting stronger, having some time just for you and building your confidence. And most importantly, start when it suits you.

Before pregnancy, each of us had a different body with different abilities. Then we endured differing pregnancies and went through labour, and we all know how unique that experience is! Reintroducing exercise and eating plans needs to be taken slowly, I don't feel like a "ripping the bandaid off" approach will serve you or your little ones.

After all you have been through, it makes sense to let your body have some time to rest. You'll know when it feels right to get yourself moving and grooving again.

Some cultures still enforce that mothers be on bed rest for weeks after childbirth to allow their bodies to fully recover from the experience. That's probably not an option for all of us, but the idea is there.

Having a newborn doesn't allow for us to focus on superficial concerns about our bodies – this time is for us to just be with our babies and our families. As the kids get older, their needs change… but from my experience the time and dedication required doesn't change all that much.

We think each phase gets easier, *hmm*, not so sure about that one. Move forward with kindness and no pressure towards yourself. Forget what you're seeing on social media, that is a toxic vortex all unto itself.

If you can stop focusing on having negative thoughts about your weight and appearance, you might just be able to acknowledge that your body has achieved the most incredible feat it possibly could. Give yourself some space to relax and stop worrying about your amazing comeback transformation right now. Don't try to bounce back at six weeks, don't lay the expectation that your youngest is four and you should be better than this. Focus on what feels good for you and what you can manage.

Now after birthing three babes into this world in four years, my body looks how it should. I have soft bits, some parts don't work as well as they used to, many things have dropped and all of this is okay.

My relationship with my body is a constant work in progress. Some days I love every bit of her, amazed at everything she continues to endure. Other days I cry in front of the mirror. Those days are the worst. Being uncomfortable in your own skin has to be one of the most horrible feelings. But afterwards, I acknowledge this is my shadow and there is space where I can choose to invite love in.

You are the
perfect creation

Everybody has a part of her body that she doesn't like,
but I've stopped complaining about mine
because I don't want to critique nature's handywork…
My job is simply to allow the light to shine out of the masterpiece.
— ALFRE WOODARD

I had this horrible feeling in the pit of my stomach. We had a thing. An event. And I hadn't seen anyone in such a long time.

I stood staring at my wardrobe hoping that whilst gazing I would find a dress that made me feel more like me, that covered the bits I despised and made me look skinny.

Or at least, not fat.

I tried on everything a dozen times and was gutted each time, especially when I didn't even feel good in my fail-safe dress. I couldn't feel good about myself, I felt defeated, embarrassed and ashamed that I had put on so much weight.

I moved to the bathroom and stared in the mirror analysing it all. Tears welled in my eyes as I longed to see a body I loved; one I could accept.

As I started to imagine all the things I would change and make "better" I heard a tiny whisper at my feet.

"Mum, why are you crying?" My tiny little Ruby gazed up at me with innocent eyes.

My tears flowed heavier, partly because that's what happens when someone, three-year-old or not, witnesses your feelings, but also because I felt so disappointed. She was watching me hate on myself – the one thing I never wanted for my daughter.

I always hoped for Ruby that she will be confident and love her body. That she will not hand power over to the male expectations on women and she will be a liberated goddess. In that moment, I could not have been further from that truth.

The female body is something else. A woman's body is so unique with the miraculous ability to carry and nurture our babes into this world. It has been created perfectly to be a mother.

I want you to acknowledge the miracle that is your body. Those stretch marks and spider veins, that weak pelvic floor and aching back are all signs of the pressure your body endured while loving and carrying your child. Your receding hairline (I thought this only happened to men!), adult acne, larger than life nipples and non-existent abdominal muscles are proof that you recently birthed and cared for a baby. Your back pain, sore neck, frazzled and dry hair, dark rings under the eyes, hairy armpits (and hairy everything, mind you), dry and split fingernails, and extra kilos are all indications that you are continuing to tend to the needs of your children.

Being responsible for the wellbeing of another human who is so dependent on you means a lot of physical sacrifice for your body. We all know deep down that those physical attributes listed above should be worn with pride, but we are up against our own egos and stories passed down through society that use a spotlight to focus on and pick apart all our "faults".

Your body created a miracle each time it nurtured and then brought your little ones into this world. It continues to do so each and every day, so don't make the mistake of assuming that because you feel tired, weak and broken, your body isn't working hard every single moment of the day.

When I was a massage therapist, the most common condition I saw in mothers was what I kindly referred to as mother's back, characterised by pain in the lower lumbar region of the back and across the back of the shoulders and neck. It is usually caused by lifting and juggling a baby in one arm while simultaneously holding the hand of a toddler, trying to put two oranges in a plastic bag as you hunt for your purse and try to answer your phone when it rings!

Motherhood puts our bodies under pressure and strain. We hunch when we breastfeed and are forever picking up toys or carrying kids' schoolbags, pushing overloaded prams and bending down to their level, all of which compromises our posture every day.

We push ourselves past the point of being tired because taking a moment to rest and rejuvenate actually is one of the hardest things to do.

We often may feel like our bodies are working against us and become our enemies. It can feel like we try to do all the things and nothing works. We don't look better; we don't feel better. Nothing is working is often our spin on it.

Post-babies there are a lot of things that our bodies have to contend with to keep balanced. Our stress levels are often incredibly high, we have hormonal irregularities, we are more prone to issues with our thyroid, circulation, pelvic and core weakness, and neck and back pain.

It may seem like it's futile, but our bodies truly are always working with us to better our health.

My health has never been the same since the birth of Ruby. It's one thing after the other. Lots of confusion, chasing leads and doctors and herbalists in all directions.

And let me tell you, when you don't have your health... you feel like you have nothing.

I'm not sure I'm closer to resolving my issues with hormone imbalance, severe premenstrual symptoms and debilitating fatigue. But I am closer to accepting this as it is.

I've exhausted myself trying to fix all the things, because mamas are the best kind of fixers, right?

The most peace I have had is letting go. Surrendering. Trusting that my body has its own innate wisdom to heal. It can and it will. It just may not be to my schedule.

Surrendering to anything in life is the greatest spiritual lesson. Letting go and trusting the outcome goes against most of our DNA. We fear the unknown.

But I didn't have an option. I had to accept my body's perfection in its own creation and trust I would heal or I would continue down the same path of depletion I had been on for years.

Sometimes "trying" so hard to do all the right things and fix or better ourselves makes us worse. I haven't stopped my self-care, I've just streamlined. I listened to my body and followed what was most important.

I'm back taking my antidepressant because even though I wish I wasn't on it, it helps me be at base level more often. Without it I start the day drowning and try to come back from there. I take my nutritional supplements daily to make sure my body is supported so it can be in an optimal state. I get support from my psychologist, kinesiologist and naturopath because trusting my body doesn't mean I walk blindly, it means I am guided by those who know best. I feed my body with nourishing foods, exercise regularly (in a way that feels good with no pressure) and meditate every single day.

This formula works for me. It may not solve all my health problems right now, but it's giving me the best baseline to start from. Most importantly, it feels good for me. You need to listen within and find the perfect cocktail (no, not a margarita) of healthy self-love that works for you and your body.

Minimising the load and surrendering to my body's own wisdom has brought me great peace. I know I'll get there, and you will too.

Re-loving you

At its heart, re-loving yourself is all about awareness and acceptance.

So many of my experiences are related to my disconnection from self, so much so that all aspects of my life were being affected.

For too long I let these stories from my past and present shape my self-belief, until eventually I realised that the only way to truly re-love myself was to take responsibility for my life and look at myself with loving eyes, no matter what situation or circumstances I may be in.

I had to give the same love to myself that I reserved for those I care about. Until I could do that I would just continue to cycle through the same patterns and get stuck in the same thoughts over and over again.

Re-loving yourself is about accepting all that has changed, good and bad, and accepting yourself as you are. It's not waving the white flag, instead it's your powerful statement to yourself that you believe you are worthy of love and you're willing to let the old stories go.

Self-love work takes courage and it's not a process we do once and forget about. We are constantly reminding our wounded inner selves that we are worthy of love by showing up for ourselves each and every day.

Journaling can be an incredible tool to help you discover and uncover the core issues with your own self-love and appreciation. We may not even be aware of some of the limiting beliefs we have or where a lack of self-love and appreciation is blocking the way for more love to flow into our lives.

- What makes you worthy of love?
- What experiences tell you that you do not deserve love?
- What self-limiting beliefs or stories do you buy into?
- In what aspects of your life do you feel you have let yourself and others down?
- What do you fear most about not being good enough?

Allow yourself to surrender to the feelings that come up as you work through these questions, even (or perhaps especially) when they are uncomfortable or painful. It takes courage to soften into these prickly edges of discomfort, but releasing the feelings is much less painful than pushing them down inside.

Don't forget that such moments are when the miracle can happen and you can create space for change, so go with it.

The more honest your reflections, the more you will have to work with when moving forward.

As always, take your time with this. There's no rush and no need to feel like you have to deal with everything you've written all at once. The first step is just to get it out of your head and into your journal.

Once you have got through the messy heaviness of all *your I'm not good enoughs*, it's time to start building yourself back up.

From your responses, you will be able to see the areas where you need to forgive, shift your thinking or welcome your present reality.

We are all a little wounded in some way. There is no judgement here, doing the inner work to heal yourself is a huge process that will change your life.

When you begin to understand where the cracks are in your self-love you can work on creating more love within. You will stop hating on yourself, stop caring what everyone else thinks and start living your life, your way and accepting *all* of yourself.

You are good enough

We have some beautifully sensitive kids in our home. Sent from somewhere else with an old soul, they never cease to amaze me with their capacity to love and show us life from another perspective.

I've struggled with my mental health on and off for many, many years and one thing that strikes me deeply still is the impact that has had on our kids.

Has seeing me cry and fall apart damaged them? Or has my experience taught them emotional resilience and understanding?

One thing I pray is that it's the latter. All my experiences in motherhood have made me question my worth and reflected back to me the old story that "good mothers" don't do this. Our children deserve more than this and I'm just not good enough.

One day I was sombre and upset, trying to keep it all in so the kids wouldn't see me. But Jacob, he sees everything. He disappeared from the lounge room for a while and came back with a smile and a piece of paper. His tiny little hands passed me a page filled with colour. Written across the top was *The game to make Mummy happy*. He had created a little board game with hearts and flowers all hoping it would make me happy.

Now, you could look at this like kids should never have to do this for their parents. And they probably shouldn't. But that day, instead of not feeling good enough I felt like for once I had done something right. My gorgeous little boy was showing such beautiful compassion. He witnessed my emotions and without prompting he wanted to make me feel better.

I knew that even though seeing his mummy cry may have felt confusing for him, from this experience he also knew how to be a loving and caring human.

I could easily fall back into the story that I'm not a good enough mama, that they deserve better, that I will leave them with wounds so deep, but I choose not to. I choose to believe that this journey is exactly as it's meant to be. I know I am showing up every day with everything I have. Some days it may not feel or look like that is enough, but I know it's my best that day.

I know that I've always given my children everything I have even if it meant leaving nothing for myself. I know that every time I have felt sad, lost my temper or done anything that wasn't "good enough", I always made it right. I always told them that adults have big feelings too and that crying heals the soul. And I always said "Sorry if some days it feels like I am not the best Mummy, but I'm trying. No matter what you see there is always so much love for you inside me."

Deep down, we all know we are good enough. That's why this a journey of self-discovery, it's not finding anything new necessarily, more finding what was already within you.

Then all the "stuff" that happens along this journey of life tests this inner knowing. It makes us question our belief in ourselves. It's information coming in that we need to decipher and our tools for understanding the new information are all based on past experiences and our own self-love.

We mistake the journey as negative and out to get us, convincing ourselves we have failed and aren't good enough. The journey may feel so hard and unfair at times, but it is bringing you every experience to guide you closer to a deeply connected life. Bringing you closer each time to your truest self.

As you are right now, in this very moment, Mama, you are good enough. You devote yourself to your family, you love fiercely from the deepest parts of your heart and you show up. Reading this book is showing up for yourself.

In motherhood all the *I'm not good enoughs* arise again from the mother archetype, the gold standard of what we think we should all be aspiring to be. When we are trying to do all the things and be all the things, something somewhere along the line has to give out. We can't actually tick all the boxes and give it one hundred per cent all of the time.

So, when we fall short or take the easy route or do anything that isn't what "good mothers" do we feel we aren't enough. They told us this is how you be a good mother then burned the manual.

And in some ways, thank God they did because now we can write a new one. It would say something like this: 'Dear Mother, Welcome to motherhood. Follow your instincts. Be kind to yourself. This won't be easy. But you are strong. The End.'

Motherhood will be the most challenging experience in your whole life. It asks you to bring all of yourself before you even truly know what that means and then you break yourself down and rebuild yourself all whilst nurturing little humans to their fullest potential.

Of course, somewhere along that journey you will feel like you are not good enough. We doubt ourselves when we think we are failing. But failing isn't black or white here, remember this is all experience and learning for both you and your children.

Every time you want to rest on the lounge instead of going to the park, you are good enough. Every time you say no just because it feels easier, you are good enough. Every time you wish you were somewhere else if just for this moment, you are good enough. Every time you silently cry or lose your temper, you are good enough.

And yes, every day you crack open the wine a little earlier than happy hour should start, you are *still* good enough.

- You are perfect right now, exactly as you are.
- Inadequacy, comparison and shame are normal human emotions that are driven by fear.
- Your internal dialogue needs to reflect respect and admiration you have for yourself.
- Your body made tiny baby miracles and that achievement in itself is one to praise and be revered.
- No amount of external gratification will ever replace self-love.
- It's never too late or too hard to re-love yourself, and it is always, always worth doing.

Take a deep breath, you have worked through some heavy subjects in this chapter. You should feel proud of yourself.

Do you feel lighter now? I hope so, beautiful.

Connection

Only recently, Spooner told me that what upsets him the most is seeing me intentionally changing myself to avoid a bad situation. Anxiety and depression will do this to me every time. Avoiding mothers' group, saying no to social gatherings, fearing the escalator, staying inside all the time. I'm changing. This illness makes me think I need to be alone. I'm scared to be with anyone who might be able to tell I'm hanging on by a thread. I'm scared to be anywhere that may trigger a panic attack. I'd rather be alone and safe. Spooner said I'm slowly changing, slowly giving into the fears and letting them run my life. He said I need to face my fears before they become me. Is that really where I am at right now? Fight or surrender to all of this? I've been saying for so long now that I don't feel like myself, and that I have really lost a sense of who I am. Yet every day I soften into the grip of this anxiety and depression. It feels easier to give in and let go than to resist and reclaim myself. But that pains me. I was once happy, positive, loved people and had so much to give. That feels so distant for me in this moment. Spooner is a man of few words, potent when they do arrive. If he is telling me, he is watching me slip away, then I have to do something about it.

Along your journey so far, you have reconnected with your true self and the woman you have become as a mother. Now it's time to understand the importance of connection with those around you.

Human beings are creatures of love and connection. Take away all our material possessions or tangible realities and all we seek is to love and be loved. We need love to thrive and we need it to survive.

When I became a mother, the emphasis on the relationships in my life was heightened. I went through the inevitable reclusion and solitary moments, and then ultimately came back to knowing that I feel lost without others and realising that they may feel lost without me too.

Think of all those times when you've called a girlfriend in tears, struggling to find the words for how you feel you're failing as a mother and it has nothing to do with the explosive nappy incident on your lounge that tipped you over the edge. Or the days when she returns the call by anxiously yelling into the phone about how her effing kids continue to fight all day long and if only they could listen to her, just once. (I know these words off by heart. I was in her place just a few weeks ago.)

We need each other. Our friends, families, partners and kids; every moment of connection we have with others offers us a chance to heal ourselves and each other.

Speak up

I sat slumped on the end of my bed. Defeated, exhausted and sad. I'd never felt so alone as I did in that moment.

Months earlier my Mum passed away. She was diagnosed with an aggressive form of pancreatic cancer and although she underwent treatment, we lost her just ten weeks later.

Losing a parent is a pain that bears no words. I had imagined she would grow old with Dad, the two of them a perfect match forever. That she would be there to see our kids grow up, not for us to be showing them photos and telling stories of a woman they may never fully remember themselves.

Losing Mum ripped my heart out in the most savage kind of ways. I wasn't ready for that kind of pain. I wasn't ready to feel like I was just that little bit more alone.

Our parents give us a sense of belonging like they are the framework for where we fit into this world. Without my mum as a pillar, I felt so lost.

Months later whilst sitting on my bed, the reality dawned on me again, as it does with grief coming in and out like the tide but much less predictably. I was feeling like I was drowning. Only just keeping my head above water.

We were living far from family and friends and I was just wishing my mum was around the corner and would pop over for a coffee. I wanted to be like everyone else who had their family close by. Grief can creep back in for the simplest of moments that make you wish it was all different.

But it wasn't just about my mum, I was missing everyone. The last few months had been emotionally heartbreaking and distressing for many reasons and we were also the parents of little ones with special needs.

Life was having one of those moments when I wasn't just drowning but life itself was pulling me under.

I needed help. A little something from someone, anyone, and I started feeling resentful that no one offered.

So, I sat there, wishing for things to be different, too exhausted even for tears. Defeated.

When I look back at those times, because there have been many just like that over the years, I realise one thing... I never really asked for help. Actually, I didn't at all. I kept trying to do it all myself. To prove to everyone and myself I was strong. Good mothers don't need help, they do it all by themselves. I didn't want to burden anyone and instead placed more on myself.

I needed them to help yet I couldn't bring myself to show them how much I needed it.

I was becoming resentful of those around me for not showering me with love and support, didn't they see me suffering and struggling? Didn't they understand what our family of five was going through?

But we humans are complex creatures. Often, we are so consumed in our own world and worries we can't see others. Or perhaps we see it, but don't want to be overbearing or offend anyone.

And sometimes, we see it but can't help. We are all drowning in some way sometimes.

One thing I have learned over the years is that if I am drowning and need help, I have to ask. I can't wait. Just keeping my head above water is no way to live, not for me, not for our family. I have to speak up.

Asking for help is hard. If it was easier, we would all do it and we wouldn't have as much suffering in the world.

Despite what we may think, being honest about needing help does not make us weak. In fact, it's the complete opposite. Knowing when to exercise self-care by admitting to ourselves and others that we need help is a *fearless and compassionate* act that demonstrates strength. It takes a strong and courageous person to let go of guilt and self-judgement and be willing to say they need help.

Many times over I've sworn to myself I would ask for help. I'd had one of those horrendous bottom-of-the-pit moments and promised I would never let myself get there again.

I tell Spooner I need help and I'm breaking. I may even shoot a message to my bestie that I'm not feeling great. I make an appointment to see my psychologist... then I pack it all away. I do all of those actions with no follow-up.

If anyone asks if I'm okay, I reply with a steadfast *Yes, I'm fine, I was just having a bad day/week. I'm all good.*

And we believe we are. We might even feel deep down we are, the mood swings have gone, we don't feel stressed, in fact, we haven't cried all week. So, we think we are good. We naively push aside the help, convinced we no longer need it.

The moment has passed but our need for help hasn't.

But when you're drowning, keeping your head just above water does not save you. Only being pulled out and rescued will.

We think in those lull moments that don't seem as intense as last time that we are okay. We convince ourselves we are good. Then just as life does, the ebb and flow continues on and we find ourselves again in that pit.

We need to ask for help and *follow through*. We need to look at our history of surviving instead of thriving and know there is a better way.

People who love you want to help you. Professionals are there to support you. You're not asking too much. You're honouring yourself and trying to be the best mama you can be.

The longer we put on a brave face and continue trying to assume the identity of Super-Infallible Mother, the more we subject ourselves to a build-up of pressure and expectation. Like a build-up of anything, in the end that has to go somewhere. We can either release it in a healthy and productive way or let it become too much for us to bear.

It's okay to release it, and I actually think it is essential to do so. By holding on to such pressure and expectation we risk harming ourselves emotionally or damaging the relationships that matter most to us.

Feelings may start within but I don't think they belong there. It's always better out than in and especially when it comes to keeping you happy, healthy and in a good space.

Wisdom through connection

In any encounter you have with another human being, there is always an exchange. We are inextricably linked to one another, all of us. There is an energy exchange in every moment, this could be the love that you and your partner share for each other and with your children, the exchange of monies for goods or services, or even the smile you give to a passer-by in the street.

It's happening in every moment so sometimes we may not even realise that an exchange has taken place, we don't realise the potential impact of our actions and words. We may say nice words to a friend without realising that she was having the worst possible day ever and your words gave her a reason to have hope. Equally, we may lash out and say angry words to our children without realising that they were feeling vulnerable and scared already that day.

When the kids are having a bad day, you generally feel down too as much as when someone is beaming with happiness it is contagious. The energy we exchange in our daily connections is profound.

Giving is a beautiful act and we are equally graced by receiving.

By nature, I have always been a very giving person. I was always the student to go the extra mile on a group assignment. I'd volunteer to help friends even when I didn't have the time and spent many years giving love and energy to my massage therapy clients. I still always, or almost always, prioritise other people over myself (this is my work in progress).

So, when I became a mother, the transition into *give, give, give* came very naturally to me. The problem with giving is when too much is going out and not enough is coming back the result is fatigue, resentment and frustration. (Insert picture of unhappy, tired mummy with refluxy baby here.)

Do we see, understand and even value this exchange we have between our relationships and connections? Can we see that in these moments there are lessons and wisdom?

As mothers we feel like we do so much of the giving, our energy is always being externalised and like I said that leaves us depleted and resentful. When we give all the time, we feel unappreciated and without any intention, motherhood can at times feel like the most underappreciated thing we do.

Look at your children, though, they aren't taking out of selfishness, they receive your love and return it in the only way they know how. Although your kids can't always return your love in the way you may need them to, they are always giving that love to you. We all know this. They just do it in their own way.

But our kids give us much more than love, they give us knowledge and insight too.

In my short time as a mother, I have learnt so many things from my children. I believe I am wiser in life for being a mother. I see myself so differently now than before. They have shown me I am stronger than I ever believed I could be. They have shown me that courage will be born from love a thousand times over. I am much more aware of my actions and the repercussions on those I love. I know the value of self-love and being authentic because I want them to know the same. They have shown me the importance of being present and slowing down with those you love. They have reminded me that life can be fun and joyous, even for adults.

In every connection I have in my life I learn something new. What about my gorgeous husband? Spooner has shown me how liberating it is to not care what anyone thinks or accept less than you deserve. He has also shown me the strength and flexibility of our love. It has been bent further than I thought it could go and it has never once faltered.

Spooner has taught me to believe in myself by always being the one who believes in me first. He has reminded me that no man wants to hear me whinging about my butt all day and that sexiness comes from me taking ownership of my body and loving myself always. His hugs show me how all my troubles can be swept away when I am held in the safety of his arms. He revives in me a sense of belonging when I see him playing with our children.

Every connection with our direct family, extended family, friends and colleagues teaches us something. We have the opportunity to learn from these connections we have.

If we feel overwhelmed and unappreciated either in our home, at work or in our relationships, we can choose to find love in that space by asking what has this relationship taught me? What has this person blessed me with?

At times it will be kind words and actions that reminded you of your own strength and beauty. At other times, people's harshness will actually force us to return to ourselves and use their actions as a tool for uncovering the wisdom within.

The journey to self-discovery isn't just about you and you alone, it's about all of us as one.

Look at those relationships close to you, the ones filled
with love and the ones that challenge you.
1) *What do you embrace or are triggered by with these relationships?*
2) *What has each of these relationships taught you about yourself?*

Raw motherhood

One of the most powerful ways to forge those essential connections is through honesty. I'm not sure there is actually any other way to be.

Dishonesty breeds complications. Dishonesty and hiding our truths is a lonely place to be.

Too often we hear mums saying things like *The kids are great, I'm doing fine* and *I'm tired but good*, when the reality is more like *I can't handle the kids, I'm at my breaking point, I'm beyond exhausted* and *I need help*.

This is the truth of motherhood so many of us feel but cannot bear to let anyone else know. It is hard, exhausting and testing when you are guiding human beings through life and we are all having the same experiences.

Yet still we feel divided, we hide our truth because being honest is always trailed by fear. We fear someone will respond with shock and judgement or worse still, that they can't relate and therefore we must be failing.

Speaking honestly is more than saying with an awkward giggle that you want to strangle the kids, we laugh about it often and use humour to soften the truth. (Because expressing raw emotion can feel uncomfortable when you say it, but also when you hear it.) It's about saying out loud what this really feels like for you. It's expressing the things you feel guilty for, it's sharing the frightening thoughts you may have, because we cannot heal in silence. Our healing as individuals and a collective of mothers comes from the raw truth.

What would change if we could press pause on the shame and guilt about being judged and just say it as it is? We would have mothers who aren't swallowing their emotions, who aren't drowning in expectation and mothers who aren't unhappy anymore. This way of glossing over motherhood so it's shiny, perfect and acceptable is creating a toxic environment for mothers and their families.

Mothers who are pushing their feelings down inside will have health issues, mental health concerns and they won't feel fulfilled, all of which will have a direct impact on their marriage, partnerships and their children.

The only way forward is with honesty, the raw, uncomfortable, messy truth of motherhood and what that feels like inside of us.

Sharing isn't just about freeing ourselves but it's also freeing each other. When you share your struggles honestly with another person, you open up the opportunity for them to share as well. You say to them it's okay for them to feel scared and vulnerable because you do too. When we do this, miraculous things can happen.

Honesty shows us in our rawest form and the vulnerability that comes with that is something we can all relate to. We all have feelings inside, we choose to hide and all we truly want is for people to see us for all of us. When we show that to each other we break down walls.

By being honest about such things and getting real with other mothers, you can help them explore their own truth too. It may be that your thoughts are exactly the same as a friend's, and it's highly likely that if she's not going through it right now, then at some point she has been or will be exactly where you are. If you open up and express your thoughts and feelings about your experience, you create a safe space for her to do the same.

When we are real, people are drawn to us. Showing someone your truth should not be what we are all afraid of, living a life in the dark and hiding our truth is way more frightening.

A few months after my diagnosis of postnatal depression, once I had begun to accept that this was just part of my life right now, I made a conscious decision to be open about it. No matter how uncomfortable I felt and no matter how quickly shame rose to the surface, I stayed strong and told people. I showed them my truth.

In fairness I didn't talk too much about the details of my emotions and what was racing endlessly through my mind, that felt like way too much to share and only in this book and through many years of healing and inner work have I been able to show you it all. But just saying out loud *I've been struggling with depression* was a weight being lifted in itself. The more I was open about it, the less I felt I truly needed to be ashamed about.

My narrative changed from *I'm a bad mother* to *Even good mothers feel broken.*

Every time I spoke truthfully about my experience, I took power away from the shame, anxiety and fear of judgement, and the reaction I got from everyone was very positive.

Obviously, some people were shocked and generally most people didn't know what to say – and that's okay. I never expected words of consolation. Rather, it was about me being open and proud of the journey I was on. I wanted to create some kind of positive light in the bubble of darkness I had been living in. I knew that confiding with those I could trust with my feelings was a big step to start healing what I had been holding in for so long.

Sharing my experience started to heal me and it healed those around me. Spooner and my friends were no longer confused about why I was so distant and changing. It gave another friend the chance to reach out and ask for help, my honesty about my experience made her feel safe with me. She had been experiencing debilitating anxiety in silence and until she reached out I had absolutely no idea. I hope that day I made her feel like she would never be alone in that feeling.

We are not being rewarded for holding all our emotions in and suffering in silence. Becoming this perfect mother archetype has no reward at the end. Motherhood is beautiful madness; it always will be these polar opposites.

The more we try to contain normal feelings associated with motherhood the more we enforce the unrealistic ideal of what a "good mother" should be like. If we are forever striving for an unachievable and unrealistic way to be, we will never get there. Instead, we will spend our lives filling ourselves with the heavy feelings that when not released become toxic.

Motherhood will raise so much from within the depths of you, and this is all normal. It only doesn't feel normal because we are trying to be shiny and perfect instead of real and flawed. Those normal feelings aren't bad but they become toxic to you when you don't witness them, and label them with shame.

Feeling overwhelmed and wanting to escape it all is normal. Having days when you sob on the bathroom floor from exhaustion is normal. Feeling like you are unappreciated and unfulfilled is normal. They may not feel nice but they are normal feelings in motherhood. They only don't feel normal because they happen within and behind closed doors. But we have the opportunity to change that and let our truth, in all its messy glory, become our light. This is what conscious motherhood reflects back to us. When we can apply a loving perspective of acceptance onto the most unlikeable aspects of ourselves and our lives.

Light or dark

Writing these next words feels like it's ripping at all of me, my brain is panicky, urging me not to share this. To keep these shameful feelings inside and locked away. I'm safer if no one knows this about me. However, if it's locked away, then the next mother may believe her darkest feelings aren't normal and fall deeper into her pit. But we can rise above that when we see ourselves in each other.

There have been moments since having my children when the darkness enveloped me. When those feelings of sadness and exhaustion progressed into desperation and surrender.

When you carry a heavy emotional load for some time some parts of yourself just feel like they can't go on. Like moving forward with life itself feels like way too much and you don't believe you have the strength to do so. Feeling so despondent and ready to give up on life has happened to me in two moments that I remember very clearly. What I want you, as a mother reading this to know is, feeling that way does happen to mums. We can adore our families and love them with every cell in our being, yet still feel like the struggles we carry within our souls can be too large a burden to bear.

Feeling lost in this darkness does not take away the love and light you have within for your family.

The darkness you experience does not mean you are a bad mother, that you have given up, that you are weak or that you don't love your children enough. The darkness does mean you have been carrying so much, for so long. We don't suddenly arrive in darkness.

Often women don't realise the load we carry on our shoulders and what we store within our hearts. It's hard to fathom that women can lose the will to live, that life itself can become too much to bear but it does – and this is perhaps the most terrifying part of women who are drowning. In the past, it has taken every ounce of courage to tell Spooner what that darkness feels like to me. I was terrified that his love would not be stronger than his fear that I was losing it, that I could no longer be a good mother for his children. I feared his judgement so fiercely even though he had never given me reason to feel he would judge me.

As hard as it can be, letting people see the truth within you is one of the best ways to heal. We can't hold space for the dark forever. Whether your dark is like the midnight sky like mine has been, or is easier to manage and comes and goes, either way, letting it go will serve you greatly.

We have to make active decisions every single day to choose light. To choose joy. To choose happiness. These emotions can only come to us when we create space for them. If we are bottled up with anxiety, fear, resentment and frustration then there isn't space for the good stuff.

Light is always more powerful than darkness. But don't see your darkness as an aspect of yourself to fear. Your darkness holds the key to so much within yourself. Your most profound realisations about the truth of yourself lie within your own darkness. It's scary as hell stepping into it and we will convince ourselves to do everything to avoid it, but what if the very thing you fear the most actually isn't the darkness itself but never finding your truest potential?

After Harry's birth, I got so caught up in a vicious cycle of self-judgement and endless questions racing through my mind that I completely lost touch with myself. I couldn't understand why he was such an unsettled baby and why I just couldn't seem to cope. This was my second time around, after all. I thought it would be easier.

We had many external factors surrounding the time Harry was born which all contributed to more on my mind and inched me closer to the edge.

There is no reasoning with a depressed and anxious mind. When you're in that state, you convince yourself of realities that aren't there.

I was so paranoid I was being judged. I felt like the weakest moments in my life were being witnessed by those I loved and that they could see me unravelling and falling apart before their eyes. I felt so ashamed and embarrassed but I was doing it all silently on my own.

At that point I honestly had not even considered that I might have depression or anxiety, even though in hindsight the signs were glaringly obvious. I was too caught up in the emotion and turmoil that darkened my every waking moment to have that kind of insight. The logical part of me that was necessary to acknowledge my need for help was temporarily switched off and I felt trapped.

Every day, I sat there crying while I tried to breastfeed and praying for some way to be able to calm and soothe Harry, who I felt a heart-crushing disconnection from. I felt lost, sad and alone. Because when you have a mental illness, you can be surrounded and held by everyone in the world and it can still be the loneliest place.

This one day is etched in my mind. I had been wound up all day long, with my anxiety and frantic thoughts steadily increasing. I was staying with my sister-in-law and missed Spooner, I was longing for one of those cuddles that just makes it all seem better. I phoned him, searching for a glimmer of hope, for him to defragment all the turmoil within me and tell me it was going to be okay. I needed to believe deep inside that he was right and it would all just pass. Talking to him did help, but no one else can really take away your anxiety and sadness over a phone call. The moment I hung up the phone, I fell right back into the sadness.

Days later Spooner would tell me he could hear the fear and desperation in my voice. The words I said and the questions I asked were things he had never heard from me before. "You weren't my Cath," was what he said. They rang alarm bells for him, and thankfully for me, he followed up his concerns with some research online.

While he was nervously seeking answers, I was spinning out of control on the inside. I was becoming increasingly anxious as it neared bedtime for the boys. I felt overwhelmed at the thought of doing it on my own, fearful they wouldn't settle, terrified I was doing it all wrong. The anticipation of it being hard struck fear through me. Never once in my time as a mother had I felt such a desperate urge to just leave, to not have to deal with bedtime or any of it, to just switch off and let it all go.

The turmoil and fear of those feelings led to my first ever panic attack. Like many people who have suffered one will say, I felt as though I was having a heart attack. The pounding and tightness in my chest were indescribable. The sensation then moved down to my lower back and I was frozen in both pain and fear. What was happening to me? It was like I was having an out-of-body experience; I was there but wasn't, between two worlds.

I knew in my heart of hearts in that moment that I was in more trouble than I had previously thought. Feeling helpless like that was one of the scariest feelings I have ever experienced, not being in control of myself terrified me. There was nothing left for me but to have to admit to myself that I didn't know how to move forward. Everything just crumbled around me.

I could have easily kept on trying to take it all in my stride, and had in fact been doing so for months, perhaps even years, if I was honest with myself, telling myself it would get better when I got more sleep, when the baby stopped crying, when I managed to exercise and, oh yes, once again, when I had more sleep. I would have probably continued denying how bad things were for as long as I possibly could, simply because I couldn't admit to anyone, least not myself, that I was broken and needed help.

I thought that getting help meant I was admitting failure and defeat, but that could not have been further from the truth.

This breakthrough was the moment when the light poured back into my life and gave me a chance to stand up and try again. It was my moment to decide whether to shine or to stay in the darkness.

My choice was simple: love or fear.

In that moment, when I had lost all my willpower, Spooner ever so lovingly gave me the hand I needed to lift myself out of the darkness.

I thank my lucky stars that a mutual friend of ours had this crazy idea that Spooner and I would be great together. I remember the first night we kissed standing in the pouring rain without a worry in the world. Even from the beginning I found so much safety in his arms.

The constant support and encouragement I got from my incredible husband gave me the strength to want to fight. He reminded me that light is always better than darkness. He led me through the tough days and carried me on the even worse ones.

I don't know if Spooner will ever understand the extent of what he did for me, but without him deciding to put me first, without his patience and without his constant love, I don't know how I would have even started on that journey, let alone continued.

To this day, I still can't come close to being able to express the vast appreciation I have in my heart for Spooner and loved ones. How do you thank someone for lifting you up and reminding you that your life has value? Maybe you never fully can. But my promise now is that I always try.

The process of motherhood literally burned me to the ground. Not being a mum, but all the other things that come alongside raising human beings. The cocktail of exhaustion, self-judgement, constant worry, the need to do it right and to love with everything I had all collided together.

I know now that this process was essential for me. I was so far from my truest self it was going to take some intense home truths and letting everything burn down around me to make way for my rising.

It's definitely not even close to what I imagined motherhood to be, but this was how it was *meant* to be. Struggling with mental health issues and two of our three children having special needs has been an initiation like no other. Some days the dark feels more prevalent than the light but that's just the nature of this beast. We can always see the dark clearer because we have to work and receive the light.

When I think back over our kids' early years, I feel a stabbing in my heart. How many of those special moments did I miss feeling vacant in my own mind? Did I do enough so they know I love them? Was there really more dark than light? Each of these questions is equally painful.

My memories don't always serve me that well, but I get the greatest comfort from photos. They tell me of all the wonderful days. They tell me the stories of love and light, laughter and happiness. The light was there, all along.

It's there for you too... we just have difficulty seeing it. It's there because despite our inner pain, struggles and depletion we put our children first. Their wellbeing and emotional safety have always come before our own. We made light for them even when we couldn't find it for ourselves.

You will find your light, it will shine brighter than you could imagine. When you do the work within yourself and live through motherhood with a conscious perspective the dark fades away. Your self-forgiveness, acceptance, honouring of yourself, letting go of the past and healing within are all steps that welcome light.

Every decision you make when you choose love over fear or light over dark counts. Every small decision, every baby step, every cautious and uneasy moment paves the way for your healing.

Over the years meditation and journaling have been the most powerful facilitators for healing. I love using visualisations to help me change my mindset and energy quickly. This visualisation is helpful when you feel down, stuck in toxic emotional patterns and lost in that darkness. You can also download your free audio version from my website. Link in the resources section.

Gently close your eyes.
Take in three slow and deep breaths. In and out.

Visualise yourself sitting in nature somewhere that you love.
Look around you and see trees, flowers, sand or water. Notice the
temperature. How does the ground under your body or feet feel? Can you
hear any sounds of birds or water trickling and waves crashing?

Next imagine that above you a beautiful fountain of light appears. It
almost looks like a waterfall of cascading iridescent white light, sparkling
and crystallised. Allow this light to pour over you and surround your
body. Now imagine that light filling your body, pouring in through the
top of your head and into all parts of your body. Let it cleanse you and
dissolve any darkness and pain within you. Allow this light to heal you.

Now imagine your cells are all individually vibrating with this iridescent
sparkling white light. You are now filled with light. How does this feel?
What emotions are arising? Sit with any feelings you have for a moment.
Let this light continue to expand into all of your being.

Stay in this space for as long as you need.
Know that you can come back to this light practice whenever you need.
You can cleanse yourself with light at any moment in your day.

Take some slow deep breaths in and out. Start to wriggle your toes, move
your hands and slowly come back into your body.
When you are ready, slowly open your eyes and have gratitude for
welcoming light.

Our mental wellness

There is such a harsh, unforgiving cloud that cloaks your life when you deal daily with the realities of having a mental illness.

In the depths of my depression, I was always tired – physically tired, but also tired of trying so hard, tired of thinking, tired of caring and tired of worrying. Life felt like it needed the energy I didn't have.

Experiencing mental illness can feel like the loneliest place you have ever been. You fear telling anyone what's really going on inside you because they could never understand. Sadly, many would understand because they have lived it themselves.

Mental health concerns are widespread and it's quite possibly the greatest challenge for all communities worldwide to overcome. Too many of us struggle and suffer daily and devastatingly, too many people are losing their lives to mental illness.

While the image of a bunch of loony mums stuck at home wearing dressing-gowns and downing endless pills is both outdated and unrealistic, it is true that there definitely were days or even weeks when I felt I couldn't function and if I didn't have little ones to care for, I would have fallen into my bed and not moved.

What I've come to realise, however, is that depression isn't always so obvious to external observers. Maybe it's because we hide it from everyone. Maybe it's also because we have learnt to function with mental illness, simply because we have to.

Life cannot just stop when you are raising children, and therefore many mums grieve and suffer and struggle on the inside without those around them ever having a clue about the difficulties they are facing.

Most of us will more than likely have empathy for what someone with depression goes through, but I don't think anyone who hasn't experienced it themselves can truly understand what it is like. I know I never did.

In my previous work as a massage therapist, I always had such deep compassion and empathy for any clients who were struggling with mental illness. I never judged or pitied them. I just gave support and compassion when they were with me. But I never truly knew. It can feel like your own living hell. You so desperately want to change but you can't.

If change was as easy as wanting it enough, then we wouldn't have this issue with mental health across the globe. Wanting to change isn't enough to shift the stories and questions that race through the mind of someone with mental health adversities.

- How did this happen to me?
- Why am I so weak that I can't cope?
- Shouldn't I be more resilient than this?
- What do people around me think?
- Do they think I'm unable to cope?
- Was I never meant for this role as a mother?
- Is my mental health having an effect on our children?
- Am I the only one feeling like this?
- Surely other mums don't have these thoughts or struggles...

Until it happened to me, I could never fully grasp the sadness, self-doubt and despair that surrounds someone going through depression. Along with the mental heaviness and physical tiredness, not to mention the anger that brews deep inside, it's as if your body knows something is not right but just can't fix it. The anxiety wracks at your mind endlessly night and day and all you wish for amongst it all is for you to get your life back. To be better. To feel like yourself again.

I have made a conscious decision to not hide from this dis-ease within my body because the more I hide, the more women who feel the same way will be wondering if the thoughts and feelings they are experiencing are "normal", fearing that they are alone in their darkness.

I know when I first started feeling depressed, I began searching online, looking for someone to say it was normal. I wanted to hear that I wasn't alone. I felt awful about some of the thoughts that were passing through my head. How on earth could I ever feel that way about my own children? I knew how much I loved and adored them, yet I still had moments when I didn't want to be their mum. There were times when I just couldn't face the fear of anticipating when they would require me to step up and be their mother.

It seemed so crazy that I could have such polar opposite feelings, such love for my children, yet such desperation to not be mummy, just for now. I wanted, *needed* to know it wasn't just me.

You're not alone. It's okay to feel the way you do. It's normal to have strong and uncomfortable feelings. Those feelings of desperation and loneliness, they are all okay.

I know you probably don't want to accept those feelings. Like me, I'm sure you are praying and begging that you will wake up from this tomorrow and feel normal again, like it was all a dream.

Some days I wish I could do what my kids do and give all my worries and sadness to my fluffy bunny at the end of the day. What I did do was journal them of an evening. I learned that I felt way better being able to express myself and move those intense feelings out of my body and onto paper. It didn't solve my problems but it emptied my bucket a little and took some pressure off me.

Our deepest desire as mothers is to love and care for our children and that desire doesn't leave us when we're depressed or anxious. It's still there, driving us even harder, which is why we become so critical of ourselves. We become our own harshest critic and pick apart all the moments we simply couldn't be there in the way we wanted to be.

That guilt is hard to bear. But we can't do our best when we are unwell. We can't do this alone. Mental illness does not discriminate. It is not a reflection of how good a mother you are, you had zero control over whether this would become a part of your life. I like to think of it as the unluckiest of lucky dips.

Every one of us mothers, whether we have had an experience with depression and anxiety or not, needs support. We all try to keep on keeping on out of fear of judgement or failure, when the only real answer is to look for love.

In my case, Spooner and my children are what saved me. Spooner stepped in and took the reins when I was too tired to steer my own life anymore. The mothers love for my children, my desire to give them their best life possible and to experience my life to its fullest are what kept me going. Every day I would look for love, I would relish and immerse myself in all the love our family had together – that was my medicine.

Because becoming a mother and the act of being their mum didn't break me. It was all the shadow parts of myself and society's expectations did. Being their mother didn't make me depressed and anxious, all the stories I believed about myself, lack of self-love, pressure to be the perfect mother and of course, genetics and physical wellbeing are what created the framework for mental health issues to arise.

I want to be really clear on this because being open about the deeper and darker feelings of motherhood can make it sound like being a mother breaks us apart. Yet *being* is an adjective, being a mother is something we do. It's the doing and trying that undoes us, not the title of mother itself. I am a mother and this in itself brings me a joy and love far greater than I ever knew. Yet I am also a woman who is trying find that space where motherhood is more about love than expectation.

Mothers often talk about bearing scars of childbirth and I'm starting to realise that for me, depression and anxiety are just more battle wounds to add to my list, and they are ones I am choosing to wear with pride.

Having a mental illness is nothing to be ashamed of. It's been the hardest thing I think I have had to accept and experience but I am so much stronger for it.

I look back on the worst years and I feel like an almighty goddess for getting through all that. I am stronger than I ever knew I could be... and so are you.

Coping with a mental illness shows us that we are strong. You may feel weak, but just being able to get through each day speaks volumes for the calibre of your human spirit. You are not broken in any way, and nor should you ever feel that you are inadequate or wrong. This is your journey.

We all struggle with letting our ego talk louder than our intuition and heart, so try to be kind to yourself, especially in those moments when it all seems too hard and you are searching for a way out or can't see past the next day. Those are the times that call for your kindness, because for each and every moment you choose love, you are inviting grace into your life. Each moment in which you can be kind to yourself, you choose love. Each moment you can be forgiving, you choose love. Each moment you seek or give support, you choose love.

Understanding and practising this has been so crucial in my own healing. For the mamas like me on this winding road of joy and depression, freedom and anxiety, I know you will get through this. Love yourself more than you ever have, you deserve your own love too.

For the mamas who have a friend or loved one experiencing this, just be there. Some days they may need you to lift them off the ground, other days they may want space. Include them in everything, tell them about your shitty days, laugh with them or sit in silence with them. We can heal mothers together.

Mama evolution

Women have an incredible capacity to love. It's built deep into our genetic makeup. We do it so well. There is power in our numbers but also in our shared awareness of a world only we can understand.

The most potent use of this understanding is allowing it to connect you with other mums. Through it, you become part of the evolution of mum crusaders who are on a mission to support, encourage, accept and embrace one another, for without this how can we ever truly unite?

If we want to break down the walls and stigmas associated with what the "perfect" mother should be, then we must begin by learning to fully accept ourselves and other mums. If we can't see another mother's pain as our own, then we aren't fully accepting her journey in all its beauty.

We all need to show understanding to mothers who are dealing with the anguish of not being able to breastfeed or the concern that their child's behaviour is becoming uncontrollable or the fear that by returning to work they are somehow neglecting their duties – even if these experiences are completely different from our own.

Kindness and compassion go a long, long way. Everyone has their own demons to face and we never know someone's story. We see their highlight reel, not always their truth. You never really know what someone else could be going through.

We can't judge or neglect other mums when we know hardly anything about their stories. Instead, we need to accept that we are all different and that we are all the same.

We're all trying to figure this out as best we can, but we don't have to do it alone.

This old, outdated story of what motherhood should look like needs to change. We have been raised to believe a story about motherhood that does not serve us. We are expected to struggle and suffer in silence as if this is a badge of honour. We are asked to let all other aspects of ourselves go because this is what pure devotion looks like. We are told that we can't ask for more, go against the grain or challenge the way it has always been because this is it.

This is why I am making a call out, with arms spread wide, to all of you mamas out there to become a Mum Evolution Crusader! I want you to stand with me and start pushing back against the expectation, the judgement and the shame we are surrounded by. We need to stand up for ourselves and for each other, and stop breaking ourselves down, competing and comparing.

We are all on the same journey and we all have struggles, doubts and fears. Rather than judging the mother who is battling her way alongside you, why not try to see her pain as a reflection of your own?

Whether it's shutting someone out in person or berating them behind their back, we have all been guilty at one point in our lives of being "bitchy". This behaviour is women disconnected from our true power. We mistake this feeling of control, intensity and pushing others down as power. This behaviour is a reflection of our own pain and insecurities.

Women who are truly powerful are empathetic, kind and graceful. They don't pull others down to make themselves feel better.

Powerful women stand together. Powerful women embrace all differences. Trying to keep others separate from ourselves is not our divine femininity.

Now, perhaps more than ever, it's imperative we stand together. We stay connected. We recreate the village we all so desperately need but lost.

Women move mountains when united. We can't expect to heal ourselves and all the broken stories of motherhood if we are unable to first heal relationships and bonds between women themselves.

I've always been a big lover of compliments, but I am even more in favour of them now. If I think a mum is doing a top job managing her son's difficult behaviour, I'll tell her he is lucky to have such a special mama to take care of him. When I see a friend who looks great in her everyday jeans and boots, I'll let her know all about it.

I really don't believe that there's any such thing as giving too many compliments. If I feel it and it's positive, I'll come right out and say it.

Giving isn't just about the receiver, I feel so good on the inside when I am nice to others.

Of course, the opposite also applies here. We need to be mindful of the effect our words can have on others.

Whether we like it or not, our world is online. Online talk is very easy to hide behind and you have absolutely no idea the impact that comments you make will have on the person sitting in front of their computer.

If you ever feel the urge to post a strong opinion about someone on social media, stop yourself. Before you join in on the bitchy conversation at mothers' group, just pause for a moment and reflect. Behaviour like this serves no one.

You're entitled to your own opinion but if you don't have anything nice to say then don't say anything at all. I believe it's a dangerous act to step forward with an opinion without knowing the full story and with no concept of the potential ripple effect that it could have in someone's life.

I vividly remember the gut-wrenching feeling that swept through me when I heard one mother's opinion on mental illness. She had a very strong perspective that anyone can "just snap out of" that kind of behaviour. She had no idea that I was personally dealing with a newborn alongside my own internal anguish on a daily basis.

I felt so much shame. In her presence I bought into the idea that I could change my reality with a flick of the switch and the fact that I hadn't made me feel pathetic. Her comments twisted me up for weeks and resulted in me placing so much additional pressure on myself and then avoiding mothers' group catch-ups for a while. I just couldn't bring myself to be around her again.

It took me a while, but in time I reconnected with the knowing that if anyone could just simply turn that switch off, we wouldn't have a mental health crisis worldwide. It takes a long time of committing to your own wellbeing to heal… and no matter how much I wanted one, there definitely was not a switch.

It's time to end the pain and the silent suffering. It's time to overcome the isolation and segregation. It's time to start a new collective, a new way of thinking, believing and living.

If I had a legacy I wanted to leave for my children, it would be that I was part of this change, this shift in our consciousness that initiated a glorious band of wholehearted, full-of-life, soul-advocating game changers – these amazing mamas who stood united, who embraced themselves and each other for all their strengths and beautiful differences. Who voiced their truth and were unapologetic for their needs. Who made the path easier for all our children to walk these same steps with grace as parents.

On the journey we've taken together through the pages of this book, we have peeled back a lot of layers that may have left you feeling vulnerable, scared and ashamed, but following that fear came love with her unmistakable voice of acceptance, kindness and appreciation.

You know those parts of the book that have resonated with you or exposed some home truths? Talk about them. Whether it be with your partner, your mother, your friends, other mamas. Share your experiences and insights and discoveries, and use those connections you make to help you stay on the path of love.

The rawness within you probably reflects the rawness in another mother who is desperate to hear she is not alone. You can help each other.

All those things you wish you could scream from the rooftops in desperation and all the things you keep bottling up inside for fear of judgement, they all need to come out, because when they do, they lose their power and you in turn feel empowered.

Decide now that you won't ever isolate yourself in your own doubt or fear and won't let other mothers do so either. Instead, be there for each other. Be each other's strength.

Together we are stronger than we are alone.

Part III

Grace

Embracing

So, I guess this is it. This is what my life is destined to be. This is what being a mum entails. It's not an easy job and it was never going to be. I feel defeated when I think about the crazy, mundane and uncontrollable life that is motherhood. Toddler meltdowns at shopping centres, sibling fights, repeating myself incessantly, crying from exhaustion, praying every day for just a little more sleep, every word I say being met with backchat and resistance, having to pin a child down in a car seat just to safely buckle him up, saying no and no and no and doing it all over again tomorrow. This is all part of my life. It's crazy, wild, mad, loud (so loud), exhausting, unrelenting and head-banging-on-the-wall kind of stuff. But I do love it. Without it, I couldn't have them. They don't come as beautiful beings of love without conditions – they are a package deal. If I want my heart to be so full of love and if I want the teary proud moments, the laughter at their silly comments, the cuddles and kisses, well, then I have to take it all. The love comes with the madness. You can't have the beauty without there first being a mess.

I can see this now. I can see that the more I bend and flow with all that mess, the more chances I have to see the beauty and the love. I suppose that should make me love the madness? Maybe not. I'll probably hate the madness just as much as always, but at least now I can see I'm strong enough to withstand it, and it won't ever break me. It will only ever make me stronger and wiser, which is why I can endure the mess. I accept the challenge because I know the reward is worth every single moment.

After all the years of working through the stuff, wading through the shit and trying to understand why this was all happening to me, why life was so unfair, I can see it now. The work gave me a new perspective. This journey of motherhood has been hard for me, that's one thing I will never gloss over. But when you know hard you then know good.

Having all of these experiences during motherhood challenged me to find myself, to find a better way of living in my own mind and heart so that I could then be the best mother I can be. Part of that journey is not actually trying to change motherhood but to work with it. To bend and flow instead of resist and control.

I can't change many aspects of being a mama, but I can change how I respond, what I expect from myself and how easily I accept myself.

I can always choose love.

Welcoming grace

Regardless of how fortunate we are, our lives will always contain some form of struggle or challenge that forces us to reflect on what is happening around and – more importantly – within us. Some of us may experience this as mental illness, while others will suffer loss or be rocked to their foundations until they finally seek stillness.

For many, parenting itself is the catalyst that forces us within.

The role of being a parent will test you, strain you and enlighten you and it will break you. But not completely.

The reflective journey you have been on throughout this book is the very same path that I walked. I asked myself the same questions, had the same doubts, held the same fears, and nursed that same longing for balance and peace in my life.

My Welcoming to grace has felt like a burning down of my old self right to the ashes so that the truest me could be reborn again. My journey with depression and anxiety, having children with additional needs, the grief of losing loved ones, all of it and more has helped me be reborn.

And still, I need to actively welcome grace into my life in each and every moment.

Welcoming grace is a choice, it's a way of life, not a destination. Everything good takes a little effort, and you know deep down that the reward for all the work and reflection you have done is a lifetime of gifts. These include being present with your family, loving the skin you are in, standing in your loving power, owning your decisions, respecting yourself through self-love and tenderness, and having fulfilling relationships with your loved ones as well as a deeper relationship with yourself.

That's got to be worth it.

Daily mum life

I remember working with a massage client years ago who was pregnant with her fourth child. She was the epitome of the woman who loved being pregnant and was in turn loved by pregnancy. She was bouncing around with so much energy and she even had red lacy underwear on, not a cotton comfy in sight.

She told me she'd had so many people give her their opinions about why she was crazy to have a fourth child, but her response about life as a parent really hit home for me.

She said: "My life changed the most when I went from having zero to one child. Anything after that is just a case of adjusting to the amount of madness in your life."

That lacy-pants-wearing woman was right. No amount of warning or preparation can help you adjust to the moment when you become a parent. Things that were never things you knew even existed become a huge deal. Your life is dictated by little people for a while and you will bend over backwards and stop at almost nothing to make life easier for everyone involved.

A daily nappy change becomes an ordeal, worrying about whether they have enough blankets or too many blankets, repeating yourself, repeating yourself again, fighting against back flips in the car seat or pram, being late for everything, becoming paranoid about silence (because something must be wrong), embarrassing meals in public whilst children scream, having disjointed and interrupted conversations, endlessly searching for an item every single day, being asked life-altering questions whilst you're on the toilet, picking up toys, vacuuming, becoming a professional chauffeur and eating on the run. I know you feel me.

This is that madness of mum life we are all accustomed to. It all seems standard and like we should just be able to accept that this is how it is and move on. But this is unrelenting and it's stressful. It's lots of small things compounding on an already stressed mother whose plate is full.

Small things become big things. And you're not a bad person for flipping your lid spontaneously at any given moment.

It's this stuff I want to hear more about, the madness, the wild times and the utter confusion over just how the heck these events unfolded. If we can laugh together, we can cry together because I want to know that your daily life as a mum directly reflects my own crazy household.

I want to know there are days when you cry too because there simply isn't any other option left to you. I want to know that there are days when you wail *Why won't this baby just stop crying!* I need to know you have days when you simply don't know how you will get through, even if in the end you always do. I need to know that all of this is just part of a normal day of being a mum.

When I know that you and I are in this together and have got this covered, I feel stronger and can accept my life and all its madness.

We can't change the circumstances of daily mum life but we can set ourselves up to be able to cope better. All the things we have been talking about throughout this book are what come into play now.

Lowering your stress levels and emptying your plate may look like…

- More self-love and prioritising your needs
- Saying no and making space for time and presence
- Doing things that light you up

- Forgiving yourself when you're having a bad day
- Knowing you are strong enough to get through this
- Asking for support and help when you need it, not when it's too late
- Talking about your feelings as they arise, without a filter
- Reminding yourself over and over that you're a good mother

Loosening your control

You may not control all the events that happen to you,
but you can decide not to be reduced by them.
— MAYA ANGELOU

Control gives us comfort. It creates a soft, cushioning protective layer around us that says nothing will change, nothing will harm you, you are safe.

Our brain was designed many aeons ago to protect us from danger and over time we now think that controlling day-to-day situations can alleviate any life-threatening situations. But we are no longer being chased by animal predators. Our need for safety is not coming from a place of life preservation but of comfort and fear of the unknown. If we can control our environment, the people around us and even our emotions then everything will be okay. Controlling is containing and contained things do no harm.

Now the problem is, we apply this to all aspects of our lives. We feel children need to be controlled because when they aren't there could actually be hell risen on this planet. Untamed children do damage. Yes, they do, but children are wiser than we think and they like nothing less than when you try to tame their wild spirit. Hence the resistance and backlash.

Sometimes, or really most of the time, you simply cannot tame the madness that is parenting. Much as we might like to think that as a mum we are organised, functioning and doing everything right, that feeling of wanting to control everything goes against the natural flow of life.

This is because control is just another form of fear. In this case, it's fear of the unknown, change and letting go.

We can't control a whole lot in our daily lives, but we damn sure try because we believe that by controlling the situation, we can somehow make ourselves happier, more peaceful and less stressed.

The alternative to letting go of control often comes with a whole host of scary potential outcomes. The behaviour of our children can change from loving and happy to a temper tantrum or teen-angst door slam in a split second with the result that our scheduled day never goes to plan and our emotions are strung out on a haywire. Our own behaviour cannot always be controlled either because we can be so easily swayed and influenced by our external environment, sending us into a tailspin.

Ultimately, as much as it may pain this mummy to say it, we cannot control anything. We can strive to manage the flow of our day and our mood, but as soon as we try to control things we are siding with fear and blocking the potential for possibility.

We need to feel secure that things will run to plan and we will remain safe from pain. In contrast, when we can release the need to control, we naturally allow more peace into our lives because we no longer associate stress, fear, anxiety and disappointment with the lack of control in our day. We don't *need* to make everything go our way and can instead accept that this is how it is and how it's meant to be, whether we like it or not.

Without needing to be in control, we don't get as disappointed about things and can therefore discover more peace and happiness.

When I talk about letting go of control, I'm not saying don't care, be lazy or break commitments – although it is okay if we do these things sometimes. The world around you will not stop spinning if your perfectly planned day with your perfectly behaved children and your perfectly stable mood somehow ends up being so "imperfect".

When we can stop associating immaculate bathrooms and drama-free days with success, then and only then can we live in the now in this very moment, right here. We can spend all our time regretting and wishing for a different past or worrying about and trying to control the future, but no amount of regret or anger will change our past and nor can endless worrying change future outcomes. The only place to be is right here, right now, with no control. Full surrender.

The more things don't go our way, the more we resist. And the more we resist, the more our *reaction* facilitates more drama.

How do you respond to losing control? How does the idea of letting go make you feel? What do you fear the most if you just let go?

Loosening our grip on control can be a fearful process to begin with but it's an essential tool in making space so you can breathe a little, reduce your stress and attempt to be as mindful of the present moment as you can.

- Stop caring so much about the clock and what has to be done and when. Time doesn't have to be your enemy.
- Don't set yourself up for failure by meticulously planning out your day. Allow room for white space and hiccups.
- Take each moment as it comes. Don't worry about what potential dramas may unfold and how you can control them. Think in the now, not in the future.
- Plan if you like to plan. If it helps you feel less stressed then get out the diary.
- Have no plan and flow if you like to flow. Trying to be structured when it is not your nature won't work.

Saying no and making space

Mothers feel obliged *all the time*. We listen to all the shoulds and follow them, and if we don't, we feel guilty. To avoid feeling guilty we just try to do it all instead.

What this actually is, is a blurring of personal boundaries and it's prioritising everyone else's needs over your own wellbeing. It's saying I am not deserving enough of doing something for myself, my needs aren't important and my own wellbeing is secondary to all else.

It's safe to say that assertiveness is not a trait I would ever consider labelling myself with, and I'm okay with that. I've resigned myself to the fact that some people are good at creating and maintaining clear boundaries in their lives, then managing to get others to respect those boundaries.

Me? Well, I'm the person who everyone loves to have around. I never know how to say no, like ever. I could be snowed under with a mountain of everything but if someone asks me for a favour, then the answer is always yes, even if my heart is saying no.

The majority of the time I actually do want to help, attend or provide whatever the person has asked for, but I simply don't have the time or space for it in my life. So instead, I compromise my own needs and place extra stress and pressure on myself.

And when you're someone like me who doesn't actually cope with extra stress in their life, then you're harming yourself. You will burn out, become resentful and feel unfulfilled.

How we look after ourselves determines how much potential we can squeeze from life. If I'm not practising self-care by setting and maintaining boundaries that give me time and space to do the activities that make my heart sing, or even just getting enough downtime for me, then I'm going to have a pretty hard time attempting any kind of growth or expansion, let alone managing all the things I need to on a daily basis.

Learning to work with these boundaries can be difficult, however, especially when it comes to our social obligations.

Glennon Doyle articulates this so well in her book *Untamed* where she refers to us trying to ease their boredom: 'As a result we are raising a generation of writers who will never start writing, artists who will never start doodling, chefs who will never make a mess of the kitchen, athletes who will never kick a ball against a wall, musicians who will never pick up their aunt's guitar and start strumming.'

We fill our kids' lives with commitments and busyness because that's what we are accustomed to doing. We hand them our phones because we are too busy and exhausted to be present.

We don't need to feel guilty about it, we need to change it.

I don't want my children learning that busy is the only way. That stress is normal. That presence in the moment is what they will spend their whole lives trying to find.

Families rely on holidays for their solid dose of quality time because they simply don't have enough of that in their everyday lives. Even when our plates are loaded with work and motherhood commitments, we still keep saying yes… when our soul is screaming no.

We are trying to have jobs, families, friends and fun experiences but it's like we are in a mad rush to do it all now. We have lost the simplicity of life and seem to accept that we can have that on our yearly camping trip but outside of that, daily life is about less presence and more doing.

When we say yes it needs to be a wholehearted yes. Yes means that even if it makes you busy it also fills your heart with joy. Yes means that doing those extra sports for the kids doesn't add stress but is filling their cup with an activity they love to do. Yes must feel good.

When we look at our commitments, we need to first assess what has to be done, the everyday stuff that needs to be done i.e., work, school drop off. Anything outside of that is a choice and needs to be reassessed if you want to create space to heal your mind and be more present with yourself and your family.

We need the joy in life, kids need to build relationships and we do need to push and strive at times to achieve our dreams. But it should never be to the detriment of being present.

I'd like you to step back for a second and think about all the things you have committed to do in the coming week. How many of them do you really want to do? How many of them genuinely nourish or excite you? How many of them are essential to your child's development? And how many of them did you say yes to when you would really rather have said no?

Think about the places where your unwillingness to say no lurks.

- When do you feel the most overwhelmed?
- In what situations do you feel your stress, anxiety or worry escalate?
- Which events or activities do you find yourself resisting the most and why?
- Which events and activities do you truly look forward to and why?
- What do you really wish you could say no to?

Letting go of our obligation to say yes to everything opens space for all the joy in life. We don't have to be busy just because the world around us is.

I believe one of the greatest lessons for our generations and those to follow is to connect back into the simplicity of life. To do more that feels good and less of what we *have* to do.

Embracing change

If you change the way you look at things,
the things you look at change.
— WAYNE DYER

It's a simple as this: when you become a parent, your life as you previously knew it no longer exists. That may sound kind of dramatic but I know you're nodding your head.

As we have talked about, that change is for the better. We become better humans when we embark on the journey of motherhood, we are given the greatest opportunity to find our truest self. But that journey isn't easy and we can resist and long for a time when everything was much easier.

Some days, it can be a real struggle to accept the beautiful madness of motherhood.

Finding peace with change will ease so much of your anxiety and worry because life will always change. Whether it is the big transition into motherhood, a career change, moving house, your children's behaviour, the dynamics of relationships, your internal landscape, it is all open to change. And it will.

We don't like change all that much because it takes us out of our space of comfort, we like where we know things. We like things to stay relatively the same with just a dash of excitement here or there. But change will happen with or without you accepting it, it is a force of its own so either we learn to embrace it or we hate the entire process.

Other times we want change so much and we don't know where to start. We long for a different feel to life, we long for something more than what we have right now. We want this change so much but it can feel too hard to start the process because we need to face up to those self-limiting beliefs. We feel selfish to ask for anything more or different than what we have. We don't believe in ourselves enough to take action. We worry about others and prioritise their needs over our own.

If we don't work through those feelings blocking our way we won't ever initiate change, we will stay uncomfortable in the comfort of how things are.

Trust that you have an inner knowing deep within you. This fountain of knowledge is in all of us and it guides us on the right path.

Some people may refer to this as intuition, an inner guide or your higher self. The title you give it is irrelevant; it's the meaning behind it that matters. This is you, your deepest, truest self. It is that divinity within us, the magical part of all humans we don't fully comprehend.

We can tend to lose touch with this self over time, especially during stressful periods in our lives, but reconnecting with it means trusting that we already have everything we could possibly need within us. It's all there, just waiting to be utilised to its fullest potential.

When you are facing and embracing change, trust that you have experienced enough in your life to have filled your well of expertise. And if you don't know what to do yet you sure will after this experience. Life will never give you anything you cannot handle.

As well as trusting this rich inner wisdom, also trust that you are already perfect as you are, that you deserve happiness and that you can make change happen.

Without trusting and believing in yourself, the process of making life-changing decisions can become tiresome and overwhelming. It can be all too tempting to back out of such decisions when they get too hard, but if you remember that you have all the answers you need within you, then you can stop looking externally for a quick fix or an aha moment. You are more powerful and capable than you can imagine and the only thing holding you back from whatever you wish to achieve and manifest in your life is you.

Fully embrace change in all its forms.

To take steps towards happiness, we need to embrace each individual change for what it is, *no matter what it is*. We need to see that every experience offers us the opportunity to grow, because on any journey to self-love and happiness there will be plenty of growth happening.

A willingness to change is wonderful but that change may not always appear to us in the form we might think or like. Our willingness to embrace it regardless is what opens the gateway for happiness and joy to flow into our lives.

The old saying that everything happens for a reason can be applied here, as each event is given to us in its perfection for a purpose. We can't pick and choose the lessons that will spark change in us, so the sooner we learn to embrace all forms of change, the closer we come to welcoming happiness into our lives every day.

When faced with a challenge, adversity or a complete detour on life's path, always ask yourself what you could potentially gain from the situation. Is there an opportunity here for self-reflection and looking inwards? Will this give you information, time or new connections that were not there before?

The lessons in our lives aren't always immediately clear to us, but hindsight gives us the ability to look back on a situation, no matter how awful it was, and see that we have come out on the other side safer, smarter and fiercer. In the midst of adversity and change, however, we can't see the eventual outcome, and so fear and self-doubt can emerge.

When an opportunity arrives for you in the form of a challenge, do your best to see it as just that – a potential opening for your soul to grow and for you to become stronger, more determined and more insightful.

Gifts in life can be disguised in the most unlikely of packages, it's not our job to judge the package and deem whether it's worthy of opening. We open it anyway. We step in. We surrender and trust that no matter what this is, it is exactly how it should be.

Implement change even when it feels hard to do so.

The action part of change is the hardest because we have all those self-limiting beliefs telling us all the reasons we should remain in comfort and not challenge anything.

Humans are way stronger than we give ourselves credit for, mothers perhaps more so. We are conditioned in motherhood to be adaptable. Everything changes on a daily basis. We become resilient and resourceful just by being mothers. But those daily decisions and changes that require strength feel like nothing when it comes to returning to the workforce, studying a new course, asking for more support, raising issues in our relationships or taking care of our own health and wellbeing.

The only way through is to act. We must take action and know that we are strong enough to bear any storm that may come our way. We are wise enough to also know that not every storm is as bad as it seems, that living in a trapped box of expectation is worse than the initial side-effects of making change.

Learning and experiencing life lessons is no good to us if we can't turn them into a positive shift in our behaviour and thinking. Knowledge is only the first step, and we must apply what we learn in order to create change in our lives. Freedom and power come to you once you initiate action, so take that leap of faith and trust that change is unfolding.

It may be that an exciting new chapter in your life is just around the corner or perhaps things are perfect exactly as they are. Either way, believe that everything is happening as it should be and take the actions you need to go with it and flow into it.

It's your responsibility to own the outcome of your life. You are the only one who can make those changes happen.

It takes strength to be a parent and courage to face up to the challenges life throws at you, but have no doubt that this strength is in you and it shines through you. It's got you this far and it will help keep you going too.

Embracing rather than resisting the beautiful madness of parenting is what allows you to really access your true strength as a mum. It's not about trying to control or perfect anything, but rather being mindfully aware and conscious of what is happening within and around you, and learning to move gracefully with that.

Although it may seem like the mayhem of motherhood has swallowed your life, it also holds you lovingly in the best of ways, so be content and at peace with the changes it brings.

Go bravely on this wild ride. Accept that you're doing a great job and know that your children are blessed to have a mummy like you who cares so deeply, loves with all her heart, and embraces this gorgeous, messy madness because she knows her life would never be as rich, as full or as joyous without it.

Expanding

I read a quote today in a magazine and it really resonated with me. "The Universe always has my back." Sometimes I lose touch with having faith in more than I can see. Having absolute inner certainty that comes from really feeling there is something bigger than me and more whole than any of us. Those moments in life when I have been fortunate enough to be able to feel my connection to that are quite indescribable. It's a real sense of being totally loved 100%. No questions, no conditions, just loved. Today I've been reminded that this sense of love is still there. I'm still being watched over and protected. I am exactly where I need to be. Everything will be okay. Today is a good day, because I truly believe it. I know this isn't all there is for me and I can hardly complain because so many have it so much worse. Yet still it feels so deeply hard some days. And I know there has to be more. My path has been set out for me to explore and it will eventually lead me to that rainbow at its end. I can feel the strength growing in me every day and I know not all days will feel this good, but I know for the first time in a long time I believe that good things can and will happen.

Life has this interesting way of testing our strength. When you're at breaking point and you've had enough of it all, at that exact moment something else happens. It's enough to make you feel like the world is out to get you. Surely it must be.

I could tell you that everything happens for a reason and there is always a bigger and higher plan for you. That this trying time in your life is here to help you learn and grow and sure, that's all true. But in the midst of teetering on your breaking point and a full-blown crisis it's also the last thing we want to hear. Nor is it what we are ready to hear.

When the going gets tough and we are challenged, some of our less desirable and more uncomfortable traits come to the surface. We become impatient, we are angered more easily, we become resentful and we may even turn nasty on our loved ones. We can't cope with everything; our stress rises and we again start operating in survival mode. We don't have the space to welcome in patience, foresight and understanding so we are left with an externalisation of the stress and turmoil we feel inside.

Having these feelings I think makes us stronger, it lights the fire in us, it shows us what we are passionate about and how we don't want to feel and inspires us to find solutions. Humans are many wonderful things but resilient has to be pretty close to the top of that list.

Your inner strength

When we are forever having to show up in life time and time again, we may not feel strong at all. In fact, the process of building strength makes us feel more like we are struggling than winning the battle. But strength is a skill that builds slowly over time. In the everyday decision to choose love, you build more inner strength.

Strength is always within you from the beginning, it's not like some of us are strong and others are weaker. We all have strength, some of us just need it to be woken and realised.

Over the years I have watched our kids go from strength to strength. It's hard for me to imagine that once Harry couldn't speak more than ten words, had several meltdowns a day and struggled to make eye contact. We have watched him grow into the most incredible little man. I can already see that his journey has made him stronger, his personality has this resilience to it, like an inner knowing that he has got this. He is one confident little dude and will give anything a red-hot go.

It has been the best kind of feeling as a parent to see Harry – once so timid and trapped – flourish into the truest expression of himself.

It reminds me that when we watch our kids, we see so clearly how challenges build strength. How the small experiences in their lives like learning to ride a bike, making friends or struggling with maths at school all help them become stronger.

For mamas, it's much the same. Our journey of motherhood does pull us into deep self-transformational work but it also gives us opportunities daily. The kids may have been sick all week, you might've notched up a grand total of five hours of broken sleep each night, you might have rocked and bounced your baby to the point of bouncing you both right out the window, you might have a deadline at work the same week the kids are having friend and boyfriend troubles at school. You are time-poor, overwhelmed, exhausted and needing a good deep chat with an even deeper glass of wine in hand.

Mothers don't realise that the everyday load on a mother is building our strength and very few of us will ever be willing to admit we are actually strong and powerful women. That might sound too brazen and up yourself. But we are. All of us. Stronger than we realise. Braver than we know.

This thing called motherhood does not spit you out the other side a weaker version of yourself, no, my love, it awakens that powerful and strong woman within whether you are ready for that process or not.

- I've learnt that I am far more resilient than I ever knew.
- I've learnt that despite what I think, I will always get through it.
- I've learnt that the faster I am willing to feel my feelings, the sooner I can begin to move forward with hope.
- I've learnt that recognising strength comes from within not from outside of yourself.
- I've learnt that my love for my children will overcome any challenge.
- I've learnt to dance in the rain and look forward to the rainbows.

There is a tiny catch here though... I feel damn sure about how strong and resilient we mothers are but I don't want you wearing that as a badge. I want you to feel proud of yourself but we don't need to translate our resilience as a benchmark for whether we are a "good mother" or not.

Strength and resilience are wonderful traits when we are doing the work, when we face our troubles and do our best to approach them with a loving response that is honouring ourselves. Strength or resilience that comes in the form of self-sacrifice and persistence that does not honour ourselves isn't what we want to be rewarding. That mindset is what feeds back into the be it all, have it all, keep keeping on and for God's sake don't rock the boat by being inconvenient. Stay in the box where good mothers do all the right things, they just be mums and they really aren't struggling.

Struggling to the detriment of yourself and then saying *I'm strong because I have just survived* is not the same strength as *I'm strong because I made hard decisions and learned from them.*

I don't want you just surviving I want you finding that fire within yourself that comes from a life-changing journey like the one you are on. You are an active participant in your life and your strength comes from that, not from your passive agreeance.

You are strong and wise and brave. You face fear daily when you hold your children's hands as they face the harsh realities of the world.

If only women and mothers understood and deeply felt how strong they are, we would possibly be living in a very different world. Because when women know and refuse to apologise for their worth, they make great things happen. When women are in their loving power and honouring themselves, they won't accept anything less than what they truly know they deserve.

When the world starts to realise that real strength is about vulnerability, compassion, self-forgiveness and learning from your mistakes instead of hiding behind a strong facade, maybe then we will start to heal the world for good.

Healing through forgiveness

Before you can live a part of you has to die. You have to let go of what could have been, how you should have acted and what you wish you would have said differently. You have to accept that you can't change the past experiences, opinions of others in that moment in time or outcomes from their choices or yours. When you finally recognize that truth then you will understand the true meaning of forgiveness for yourself and others. From this point on you will finally be free.

— SHANNON L. ALDER

Forgiveness may be the greatest tool at our disposal, yet the hardest to fully embrace. We either can't forgive those who have wronged us, or never think to forgive ourselves for our humanness.

We can all struggle with forgiveness and rightfully so, because when we are hurt, we revert to protection. We may feel anger, disappointment, distrust, unease or sadness, and when it comes to self-forgiveness, we sometimes carry the burden of these feelings for years.

Some people can see past the hurt and simply forgive, but others hold onto the pain until it ultimately burns a hole in their heart and leaves a scar there forever.

The process of forgiveness requires us to call upon all our strength to summon that powerful woman within us so we can move on with our lives and not be held back by the past. We all understand the process and we usually know whether we can forgive others or not, but while we may be open to the concept of forgiving others, we often remain relentless and unforgiving towards ourselves.

Showing yourself the same kindness and compassion you give to others is not only a game changer in your life, but a necessity.

When you become a mum, you take on a whole new world of self-inflicted guilt trips and judgement. If you do even the slightest thing wrong, you invariably drag yourself over hot coals for it.

Many of us (and I'm putting my hand up here as a recovering non-forgiver) carry a huge weight of guilt and self-deprecating beliefs with us, and we never seem to consider being kind, understanding or lenient towards ourselves.

What do you imagine would happen if you started forgiving yourself for everything you think you have failed at? Do you think your world would fall apart? I believe the opposite is true, and your world will in fact open up with incredible opportunities.

Imagine not having to carry the guilt about your birthing process with you forever or letting go of the self-judgement that you cannot provide enough for your kids or finally being free of the guilt and pressure surrounding your stay-at-home or return-to-work choices. There is such freedom in that feeling, and the way to reach it is through self-forgiveness.

Our culture and the society around us have tricked us (well in actual fact, fed our ego) into believing that the harder we are on ourselves, the better and stronger we will become. To me, this is all backwards.

Without love and compassion, how can we expect to grow, unfold and blossom into the majesty of our own being? Everything around us is all about working harder, not asking for help, forging on, not accepting failure, and measuring our success by specific, and at times dare I say it, shallow, things in life. Accepting these directives and being hard on yourself because of them is denying your inner child and spirit its freedom.

Would you expect your kids to be bursting with confidence and enthusiasm if you spent all your time breaking them down, belittling them and drowning them in expectation? Of course not, why then do we do it to ourselves? The answer is that we are so surrounded by these attitudes and beliefs that it is hard to find a way to escape them. The "daily grind" as they call it encourages you to work hard, play hard and be hard on yourself, with no room for weakness, hesitation or human imperfection.

It's a big task to shift away from what the world around you is constantly reinforcing, but it can be done because all of those notions are simply *external* opinions. In reality, there is absolutely no reason for you to continue to be so hard on yourself. You can instead choose at any time to forgive anything and everything you need. It is your choice how you will treat yourself.

As time passes, I'm finding it easier to forgive myself. Indeed, writing this book has played a huge role in my realisation of how critical I am of myself and how much difference forgiveness can make to those stories I tell myself.

I know that with forgiveness I can accept those lazy days when I have a sink brimming with unwashed dishes and am surrounded by an endless sea of scattered toys, used tissues and kids' shoes.

On more intense days, I try to forgive myself for all my perceptions of how I thought my life would be and the expectations I have imposed upon myself. That forgiveness also frees me of the mum guilt of heart-wrenching emotional meltdowns at day care drop off, the frustration at my innocent child who has developed a one-hour bedtime routine, and the daily expectation that maybe today I just didn't do enough for them.

When I forgive, I can see that my perceived "faults" that cause me to snap at the kids, lose my temper, cry, shut down or feel like I don't want to be Mum right now are all just me being human and doing the hardest job in the world in the only way I know how.

If you're wondering what you need to forgive yourself for, then look back at list of things you feel guilty about from Part I of this book. Your journal entries will also give you great insight into the behaviours and areas of your life that are most in need of some forgiveness. Once you recognise these, try softening your attitude towards yourself with the following affirmation.

I know that I am doing the hardest job in the best way
I know how.
I forgive myself for my perceived mistakes and flaws.
I am kind and loving to myself.

To be human means we make mistakes, stumble and trip, get back up and then are humbled, we learn and thrive. This is the journey of life and it's an ongoing one, which means you will never be complete or faultless… it means you will always be imperfectly perfecting yourself through your lived experience.

Even on your last day on Earth, you will still have lessons you haven't quite mastered yet, but that's okay. It's all part of the beauty and wonder of life. That's what makes life so juicy, so worth it.

Stuffing up, working out that you stuffed up, trying a bit harder or a bit differently next time, maybe stuffing up again, and then finally working it out – that is what you are here for, and the key is to keep practising self-forgiveness and self-acceptance as you go.

Let yourself see that you are not doing a bad job as a mum, you are not letting your children down, and you are not neglecting your partner. You are doing the best you can with what you have, and every time you buy into the notion that being hard on yourself is somehow good for you, the only person you let down is yourself.

You deserve better than that, don't you think?

A letter to self

Dear Cathy,

If only you could see what everyone else sees. You have a genuine and loving heart. You are always kind and caring and hold such empathy towards those you meet. Many people have said in the past they always feel calmer after being with you. You may not feel like a good mum, but Spooner has said from day one when Jacob was born that you are a natural. Your kind heart and gentleness are a blessing for your children. Please don't measure your success by financial gain. You ran a successful massage business with loyal clients who loved the work you did. You have all the tools you need to make your own version of success. You have a thirst for knowledge and learning which can be applied to anything you want. You have been called to write, to share your story and your words to help and heal. Don't let fear talk you out of this. It's your time to shine. Your external beauty is a true reflection of your beauty and soul within. Learn to love your body. It carried, nurtured and gave birth to three incredibly beautiful children. Your body is more amazing now than it ever was before. Learn to re-love it. Forget how it was and love it for all that it is now. From now on, please be more forgiving of yourself. Please be kind and accepting when times get tough. Remember you are loved and that you have so much love to give. That love can move mountains.

I love you.

Reflecting now on that letter, I am shocked by how much it all still hits home to me. The pain that I felt when writing it is still there when I read back over it years later.

That's one thing about pain, it gets easier but we always remember it. But there is also another thing and it's about being seen for who you truly are, because it will always stir your heart and soul.

And sometimes, witnessing ourselves is the greatest healing of all. We long to be seen not only by others but by ourselves too.

Our hearts do not understand the conditions and clauses we apply to our own love for and acceptance of self. Our hearts just want to be loved.

When I was able to truly see myself for *all* that I am, it liberated me. It reminded me that my essence is pure and good regardless of my faults or how many times I fail. But also, I see how much gratitude there is in it.

At the same time, I was seeking to forgive myself for all my self-judgement I was also looking at all the elements of myself that I could be grateful for in that moment. Maybe this is part of the release and relief that comes with forgiveness. When we are no longer so caught up in judgement and guilt, we can begin to appreciate the many blessings in our lives.

Writing this letter was one of the most powerful things I did in my own self-healing journey. At the time it was confronting and incredibly uncomfortable saying all these nice, positive things about myself.

We do find it hard to say nice things about ourselves without feeling self-absorbed and attention-seeking. We could name our faults in a second, but we downplay the good things so we can stay inside that comfortable little box. We often don't even give ourselves words of encouragement and support through all the challenges that this here existence brings.

As uncomfortable as this was, it was liberating too, I never could have guessed how potent these words would become when read at a later stage.

I encourage you to do the same. Write a letter to yourself as if you were writing to someone you love, as you would to your children for instance, and pour positivity and compassion into your words.

If this were your chance to release all the guilt and judgement and save yourself through forgiveness and witnessing yourself, what would you say?

Your inner wisdom

Most women spend a lifetime trying to reconnect with the essence of who they are. All our experiences have slowly pulled us away from our truth and from our inner knowing.

Women are wisdom keepers. Throughout the ages women were cherished for their wisdom, intuition and healing capacities.

Some cultures talked about this magic of women that was never truly understood but deeply revered. Sadly, those tales became distant memories as women were stripped of their strength. They were belittled and used, degraded and subdued, excluded and deprived.

This may seem like it's irrelevant to us now because modern women live very fortunate lives in comparison to some of our ancestors. But we still have work to do.

Women need reassurance and so often will seek externally for our answers because we have lost touch with our inner wisdom.

True awareness is a gift that many of us are constantly seeking. When it comes to parenthood, I believe that awareness is not only about trying to be in the present moment no matter what chaos surrounds us, but more importantly, it is about being in touch with our own deep inner knowing.

It is this kind of awareness that can help us through the challenges we face as parents. We all have this within ourselves.

A mother's intuition can be a strong force yet sometimes it becomes a whisper often drowned out by the self-doubt and fear.

We forgot that we have this inner wisdom so we ask everyone else for help. We google, we call our mums, we call the doctor, we see specialists and experts. Yet the whisper is there, it helps us navigate the tumultuous waters of toddler tantrums in the supermarket; it's what tells us the best words to say to a love-struck and heartbroken child; it's the thing that sounds alarm bells when it comes to our children's safety and best interests; and it's the guidance that, when followed and fully embraced, leads us closer to the life we are destined for.

Staying true to this awareness and inner guidance is imperative not only for us as parents, but also as human beings.

From a mother's perspective, we need to turn down the external noise so we can tune into that inner wisdom. We may not have all the answers all the time but we rely on our own instincts much less than we should.

Our wisdom is like any muscle, you use it and it becomes stronger. You listen and your inner wisdom becomes louder.

Your instincts about your child's development, their relationships at school or when something just doesn't seem right – your gut instinct, your mother's intuition, this is what I'm talking about. The key here is to become more conscious of this awareness, to intentionally connect with it and choose to embrace it. We have to actively choose to listen to this and welcome it in.

We have enough noise and distractions in life on top of our own self-limiting beliefs so this inner wisdom may not roar loud enough for you to hear. We need to believe that we do know what is best.

No one other than ourselves has the power to dictate or decide what is best for us. Only we know our heart's truest desires. Only we know our deepest longings.

How do we hear her? We silence our minds as often as we can.

I meditate daily to help create space for my intuition or inner knowing to express herself. It has become my ritual and now I am communing daily with the wisest part of myself.

When it's been a super hard day mothering, I tune in and seek guidance. When I don't know the next step to take and I'm confused, I tune in. When I am feeling self-doubt and judgement creep in, I tune in. It gives me clarity and comfort.

Questions for your inner self
- *What do I need to know about this situation?*
- *Can you show me the next step to take?*
- *What will serve my highest good?*

Since I have learnt to listen to and embrace this awareness, my life has become so much easier. I'm not saying decisions are simple now, but they have become less difficult and more guided. My emotions still fluctuate, of course, but I'm more aware of them in the moment and have more control over them instead of letting them control and overwhelm me.

The same can be true for you. It doesn't take hard work, just persistence and a belief that it is all within you. That wise and revered woman who was your ancestor has left behind a trail of her being in your DNA. It's there to be awoken and heard.

And once you hear it, you hear grace.

Take the leap

Courage doesn't always roar. Sometimes courage is the little voice
at the end of the day that says I'll try again tomorrow.
— MARY ANNE RADMACHER

Without fear there cannot be love. Without dark there cannot be light. Without apprehension there is no realisation. Without change there is no growth.

Life is all about polar opposites, where one quality cannot have a place without the other. Our job is to know when to allow the presence of one and when it's time to welcome the arrival of the next. We can accept and surrender to our fear but we need to know when it's time to invite love.

As you move through these later stages of your journey, you may be coming up against some fear. You have reconnected with your soul. Now you're on the verge of really opening up to living from a conscious perspective as the incredible woman you always knew you were.

Being on the verge means you're so close but next you need to take the leap. No matter what your lessons and growth entail you will eventually need to act on them and take that leap.

Sometimes fear speaks before we even start, while at other times it waits until we get the ball rolling then tries to sabotage us mid-movement.

Fear is distinct for everyone. It feels different and we act upon it differently, but ultimately it is driven by the same feelings and emotions.

You know the ones I mean. They say to us:

I'm not good enough.
Who am I to do this?
I would never have the time for that.
I feel like I am asking for too much.
What if no one accepts me?
What if no one likes my ideas or the new me?
Am I scared of being hurt?

My anxiety was my taking the leap moment. Anxiety is the unreasonable, unrelenting and game-changing friend no one wants around, ever. When it arrived in my life it brought with it a whole bunch of new fears I never knew existed. On one level they seemed irrational, but at the same time they gripped me so deeply that I was consumed by them.

I had fears of leaving the house in case someone could tell I was depressed or anxious (as if anyone's opinion matters anyway). I could no longer take my kids on the travelator at the shopping centre without shaking uncontrollably and feeling like I would somehow let go of the pram and hurt them. I became paranoid about my husband leaving me or dying or becoming incapacitated, to the point that I would become a nervous, crying mess. I was convinced my kids were sick or that I was sick or that something else was wrong, it had to be.

Some days I drove into a car park and then drove straight back out again. I didn't want to go anywhere new. I didn't like meeting anyone new (which, as a social bunny, was an odd one for me). I never slept well. I had nightmares and became paranoid about people stealing our cars. I was up several times a night checking on the kids and making sure they were still breathing.

Anxiety is cruel and all-consuming. Anxiety had created so much fear in me, irrational or not, it felt very real to me. Moving through these fears and taking the leap was so immensely hard.

But I had no choice, anxiety was the one thing that really turned everything from white to black and affected how I conducted my everyday life. If I didn't learn how to push past it, anxiety would have continued to change things little by little until those new ways of being became accepted and the new norm. It was time to face my fears.

I did it the only way I knew how. When something made me feel uncomfortable, I pushed through anyway. When I wanted to leave some place, I stayed. And when I thought I'd had enough, I pushed myself a little more.

Of course, there were times I freaked out, that fear forging its way to the surface, and I had to resign. But I gently reminded myself of why I wanted to get better, for my family and our life together, so I tried and tried a little more. I couldn't live a life led by fear.

Taking the leap and facing my fears born from anxiety was what showed me I could do almost anything. I knew that leap was the scariest thing I ever did and that nothing in my life would feel as scary as that.

Often, we convince ourselves, or the fear within us does, that taking a leap is dangerous and only bad things can happen. When in actual fact, you become stronger and start building more evidence to show yourself that you really can do this.

Instead of letting my fears rule me, I flipped them around and used them as a deterrent to avoid a life of struggle and heartache and as a driver towards what I wanted to achieve.

In a way, it was the fear of my own fears that made me brave. I didn't plunge into this boldly, that's for sure, but slowly, bit by bit, I became stronger.

What I learnt from this experience is that we can sit back and wait for life to happen to us or we can make conscious decisions to become co-creators in our own lives. We can choose to have a say in what is important to us, mould how we feel and the way we see the world around us.

It's your responsibility to take the reins in your own life, no matter how wild and crazy that horse you're riding is, and no matter how little idea you have how to ride. You will learn, the horse will calm, and you will be able to take better control of the direction in which you travel.

- What leap of faith feels most scary for you right now?
- What is holding you back from facing your fears?
- What needs to happen to make this leap feel successful or good for you?
- If you did leap, what would it feel like on the other side?

Step into your loving power

Our deepest fear is not that we are inadequate. Our deepest fear is that
we are powerful beyond measure.
It is our light not our darkness that most frightens us.
We ask ourselves, who am I to be brilliant, gorgeous, talented, fabulous?
Actually, who are you not to be?
— MARIANNE WILLIAMSON

As women, we can often feel that power is something we are not entitled to have. Maybe we don't feel we have earned it, or perhaps we believe that being powerful means we are too strong, domineering or bitchy.

We have been conditioned to believe that power is aggressive and only for those with dominating personalities, but the true power that lies within all of us is not at all aggressive or domineering. It's the gentlest of convictions that means once we know who we are and what we need in order to feel fulfilled spiritually, emotionally and physically we can be true to ourselves and act with respect and love.

If you ask anyone who knows me whether they would ever use the word "powerful" when describing me, they may likely say no. I've more often been lovingly called a pushover or a soft touch and even as my boundaries become stronger I *know I can* still be true to that gentleness in me.

I can be powerful and still be the softie who wears her heart on her sleeve and who shies away from any type of confrontation, because real power is not determined by our personality traits or characteristics. It is instead about knowing and protecting ourselves in our own authentic way.

Stepping into your loving power means you can ask for what you need, speak from your soul and not be dictated by other people's needs and wants. Being in your power means you are not swayed by listening to all the "shoulds" in your head.

You don't have to become Miss Bossy Boots and start disrespecting others to step into your power. It's the complete opposite, in fact.

By acting with loving power, you not only honour yourself but you honour others as well by giving them a chance to see you for who you truly are, to appreciate you on a whole new level and deepen their relationship with you. You give them an opportunity to see you and accept you as you are *without* crossing your boundaries.

In the end, all we really want is for those in our lives to see us and embrace us with loving, open arms. We deeply and achingly want to be authentic more than anything else in this world because without that authenticity, the love and acceptance we receive loses its meaning.

Being powerful in our own lives can also open many doors of opportunity to us, because when we hold back from expressing the highest truth about who we are and what we need, we allow fear to enter our lives and overtake us. In so doing, we are ultimately surrendering our personal power and succumbing to self-limiting thoughts and actions. By contrast, owning your power allows you to welcome space in your life for happiness and peace because you have created a life in which it is not only you who knows what you want, but others around you too.

One of the things that happens when you step into this personal power of yours is that you create a magical spark in the lives of your children. We all know how our kids witness and mimic our behaviour, so by owning your power, you give them the opportunity to see you being a living, breathing expression of your truest self. If they see you acting upon your desires and taking care of yourself with authentic, loving power, it will instil in them an understanding of the importance of their own power. Standing tall and owning themselves with the conviction of who they are will become second nature to them. They will not associate power with dominance and negativity but will know it is their instrument for fostering a healthy respect and love for themselves.

Indeed, without being powerful in a loving way it won't be received well, if we are stuck in that place of fear then love driven by fear is not truly love at all.

Claiming and using this kind of power may seem frightening, and it can push us past our comfort zone as we worry about judgement and facing criticism, failure and resistance. *Will everyone accept my needs when I express them? Will I upset anyone by owning my truth?* But owning your truth and expressing it with loving power will be received in the right way and remember, when it is not, it's more their issue than yours.

Throughout our lives, we are constantly changing, moving and evolving. Our desires morph. We find new dreams, enjoy different ways to fill our free time, and begin the search for other things to impassion us.

As we move through this stage of our lives as parents, we need to allow these changes to happen. More often than not, however, we find ourselves forgetting our dreams, dismissing our desires and setting aside new ideas because we don't feel worthy of them. We believe we need to put our children first and sacrifice all else. We don't know how to prioritise our own needs *alongside* theirs so we make excuses that we don't have the time or the resources to make it happen.

The truth is that we already have everything we need, and the strongest tools for making change a reality are our belief and our loving power.

Change cannot begin until you know what you want and you start acting upon it by taking small steps to invite it into your life. You need to use your power lovingly and be true to what your soul wants.

If you need time away from the kids, then ask for it. If you want to embark on a new career or take up a new hobby, make your wishes known.

And here's the thing: being powerful isn't so much about communicating your needs or wants to those around you as it is about showing your *soul* that you hear her. Make sure you acknowledge the presence of your inner guide by telling her you are not only listening but you are ready to show up.

When you deny yourself, you are not just withholding opportunities from yourself. You are ultimately ignoring your own soul.

In an unintentional way, by saying no to ourselves, we reinforce the idea that our dreams, desires and needs aren't important and that they aren't supported. While we would never consistently ignore our children's needs and requests in this way, we all do exactly this to ourselves and often without even realising it. We call it sacrifice to make ourselves feel better. We tell ourselves to get back in the box that we try so hard to fit into because the true essence of who we are isn't good enough.

But we can use our loving power to make change. If we believe in ourselves, we use our loving power to make change and truly transform our lives.

It's time for us all to let go of the idea that being powerful holds a negative connotation for women. You are not bossy, you are not asking too much from your partner, you are not letting your friends down, and you are not selfishly choosing to put yourself before your children.

Owning your power simply means you know yourself and appreciate what you stand for.

A powerful woman:

- Listens to her inner guidance and acts upon that guidance
- Stands true in who she is as an individual
- Unapologetically embraces her authenticity
- Is not constrained by fear of judgement or criticism
- Asks for what she needs without guilt or reserve
- Says no to others when she needs to
- Says yes to herself
- Is kind to herself and respectful of her power

You owe it to yourself to be this woman. When you become comfortable with asserting your loving power, you will find a lot of things that previously caused resistance and drama in your life become irrelevant.

As soon as you're able to speak up for what you need, go after your dreams, own your decisions and be your truest self, all other distractions cease to matter as much.

With loving power comes clarity. It's when all your conviction and knowing come together and you realise you have everything you need to stand strong, go after your dreams and be the incredible mama you are.

When this loving power is integrated into your life you become unstoppable.

The journey

Today I felt nothing but an overwhelming gratitude for our children. Right now, I am holding Harry in my arms thinking about all the days that have felt hard for us. He is growing bigger every day but won't ever stop being my baby. My children all show me a side of myself that I love and also a side that I dislike, but they are teaching me how to accept myself and become a better mummy and a better version of me. They have helped me realise my true self. Ever since Harry's arrival, my depression has really kicked into full swing. He was probably the catalyst for that facade cracking and breaking to reveal the fear and pain I was living in. Thank you, my darling Harry. Thank you for being an unsettled baby who wouldn't sleep. Thank you for being so demanding that it pushed me to the edge. Thank you for challenging me so that I knew I had to heal so we could all get through this together. Without this, I wouldn't have been brought to my knees and have been able to acknowledge the reality of my situation. You enabled me to make a shift. This depression will not beat me; it will only make me stronger and guide me back home. Each day, I promise to look into your eyes and be reminded of how far we have all come, to remember the bad days and to celebrate the good ones, and to know that many more days of happiness are awaiting us. Thank you, baby.

Each and every day, I face the reality of how much every moment in my journey has changed my life.

My journey to mental wellness has shown me a pain within myself that I had never known. It reminded me that to heal myself I must love myself with fierce abandon.

The traumatic birth that contributed to post-traumatic stress disorder and mental and physical illness showed me the life I didn't want to be living. It reminded me that joy and ease are everyone's birthright and that I have more courage within than I ever believed.

Our boys, Jacob and Harry, being diagnosed with Autism, ADHD and speech and reading disorders was an emotional rollercoaster and a beautiful blessing. They reminded me that unconditional acceptance and love is more important than any other imprint I leave on this world. Every day they show me how magically individual and different we all are and how the world is a wondrous place because of it.

Losing my mum in my thirties is a pain that may never go away. But it taught me that life is too short to not be happy. Life is precious and so are those you love so don't waste a single moment. She reminded me that all mothers are just doing the very best that they can and it's all we can ever ask.

I'm way beyond the point of being angry about the cards I was dealt. I've weathered the storm and I know they are all blessings.

Those years spent questioning my self-worth, searching for

reconnection with my true self, hoping for acceptance and clinging to what I had left of grace – it was all supposed to happen exactly that way. It was meant to be tough and I was meant to break, because only then did I go searching for more.

Only when I had burned did I rise again from the ashes *reborn*.

Your beginnings

Our first step in moving forward with all that we have discovered throughout this book is to go back to where it all began.

In Part I, I asked you some questions to help guide your journey. I invited you to think about your daily concerns, your goals, dreams, and what would make you happy. Now that you have rediscovered and reconnected with your true self, I'd like you to revisit your responses. Remember that these were written when you were right at the start of your journey into conscious motherhood, so some of your answers may be a little hard for you to read over. That was a very different woman with a pen in her hand back then, so be kind and loving as you read, and reflect on whether those responses are still relevant for you.

My hope is that as we've travelled through the pages of this book together, those concerns now have your awareness. I'd like to think you have developed more faith in your ability to deal with these issues and that you've acquired a new perspective to help make those dreams a reality and bring happiness into your life.

It's possible that with your newfound confidence and inner knowing your initial concerns are no longer a problem. You may find your goals have evolved into something bigger. What makes you happy could be completely different now as well.

But please don't be disheartened if you feel your list remains the same or if you think you could add to it. An ever-growing list is a normal part of the process of self-development. Life is a constant journey.

This process is all about reflection and discovery. The more we discover, the closer we come to living and loving our truest self.

As you look at your responses, identify what needs to be done or acknowledge the progress you have made. Feel free to make notes in your journal relating to this exercise, as it can reveal how far you have come and how much potential you still have within you.

Knowing that you have already overcome your initial challenges, or can at least acknowledge you have the ability to do so, makes continuing on the journey so much easier. I know you can do it, and now you know it too. You have that inner wisdom and loving power to get the motivation happening and the self-love and awareness to keep this going.

Understanding where you came from gives you the greatest insight and motivation for where you want to be. But this doesn't have to be hard. I don't want you feeling like the journey to conscious motherhood is just another thing on your plate.

And don't worry, my self-development journey has definitely had me testing my faith in this process. "Doing the work" on ourselves can be exhausting at times. But one thing I have learned is that everything happens as it should with divine timing. I don't need to push and rush my lessons and healing. My job is to witness myself with loving kindness, always.

If you look back at the place you have come from and all you are hoping to leave behind, you may just see that you have already learnt and grown without even realising it. Sometimes that growth or lesson just happens without the actual realisation we are doing the work.

You can move forward and make positive and lasting change in your life as a mother and woman, you can take steps every day towards grace. And you will. Just every once in a while look back to where you came from, then turn and continue on with living.

Do the work in snippets. I don't actually believe that bringing the best out in ourselves is about doing this the right way all the time. We don't need to be conscious of every decision we make in every moment – but we do need to reflect with loving kindness, compassion and acceptance.

Doing this alongside the beautiful madness of motherhood is possible. I'm going to take it step by step as I show you how to stay true to your intention of welcoming a conscious perspective and embodying your truest self each and every day.

What better way to start than by revisiting our affirmation for inviting grace?

I release all that no longer serves me.
I accept what is.
I invite grace into my life now.

Dealing with setbacks

With all this new info and insight into yourself, I bet you're wondering how on earth you are going to keep all your ducks in a row every day. Well, I hate to break it to you but you probably won't, and that is totally okay, as I'm sure you've gathered by now!

Most days, my ducks are knocked halfway across the room, sometimes snapped in two or covered in who-knows-what type of sticky substance, but I know I have the tools I need to pick them up, dust them off and get them back in a row ready for the next instalment.

The reality of life in general and our mad, messy parenting world in particular is that setbacks are a given. You can do all the soul searching and self-improvement in the world, but you are still only human.

The key thing to remember when setbacks do happen is to always be kind to yourself. Remind yourself you're an incredible mama, you're doing the very best you can and never forget that no matter what happens, you always have the opportunity to choose love and try again.

The true meaning of this message hit me a few months after I was diagnosed with postnatal depression and went to a self-help guru seminar. I sat in the room nervous and distracted for most of the day, it was the first time in months I had done anything for myself and ventured out into the big, scary world. I needed to be there that day in that seat to hear all those words. You know those moments when synchronicity and divine timing come together to make sure you are in the right place at the right time? Honestly, I had never even heard of this person until a week before when I purchased the workshop ticket on a whim, with this inner knowing pulling me to do so.

She said "It's not about how far away you go from home; it's about how quickly you come home."

We will always find ourselves straying from home, from our inner truth, life does this so well to us. It doesn't even matter if you are so far from yourself that you feel lost and unfixable. You will always come home.

The more you turn inward and understand the deepest parts of you, the more you can return home quickly. That's the beauty of this kind of work.

The deeper you delve into your soul, and the more you tune into the all-knowing and caring voice that is your inner guide, the easier it becomes for you to come home again. You recover faster. You work things out quicker. You are more resilient and know the game.

Every moment has the potential to open us up. We may not always realise it at the time, but even when it seems like we are being hurled against the wall and our pretty little ducks are sprawled all over the floor, we are still learning, still growing and still opening ourselves up to the possibilities.

Coming home is about accepting where you are and knowing that this moment is just that: a moment. Just one moment in your life when things aren't pretty. If you can release the expectations you place on yourself and get right into the messiness of the moment and be okay with that, then coming home becomes so much simpler.

Don't be fooled into thinking that other people don't fall off the wagon; people who write books like this, successful women you admire, the seemingly most shit-together mum you know will still have moments. This is life.

When I face life and the unavoidable setbacks, I get in it and I get real. Whether it's feeling disappointed in myself, guilt, frustration, anger, sadness or hopelessness, I try my best to be in it fully and not hide in the corner.

I don't hide my feelings away so they can fester, only to return again much stronger. I feel my feelings. I sit in the discomfort. When I witness my feelings, they aren't as scary anymore and they lose their power. I let myself feel it and I gently let it go. Only then can I return home.

Setbacks are our reminders to check back in with ourselves. To reconnect with our loving power. Yes, we are stronger than we think and this is just a setback. Feeling overwhelmed again does not mean I am failing. Having my boundaries crossed by another does not mean I am failing. Falling into old habits does not mean I am failing.

Setbacks are like the Universe checking in, sending you little reminder to remember all you have learnt and all you already know. What is this moment showing me that I am yet to see? What could I learn from this setback? What is triggering me most here?

Remember, your power lies in your ability to turn within and reflect on what is happening both internally and externally. Because your external world will always be a reflection of your internal world.

Be present where it matters

To children, life is simple. They teach us so much more than we could have imagined and see the world with such clear and accurate eyes. Their innocence and purity bring so much passion and zest for life into our lives. They are yet to be jaded by life and all its expectations and rules. We think we are their teachers, yet they are *our* greatest teachers.

But living a life according to the rules we have been fed about fitting into that box does not allow a lot of room for presence. So much of fitting into this acceptable version of a "good mother" is an externalisation of things. How much of it is measured in just being – in our presence?

I touched on this earlier in the book and I know that the busy lives we all try to lead strip us of being fully present with our children. Yet your presence with them will be the most fulfilling of all the things you could do in life.

When you're feeling overwhelmed with motherhood and you have too much weight on your shoulders, you often want to escape.

Escapism and motherhood are very much a real thing. We want to be anywhere but here.

We think it's the kids that we need to escape from, but if our lives were less busy and we minimised our stress we could cope with our kids.

What if, when we are overwhelmed, we minimise other things in life so we don't feel the need to escape our children? What if everything slowed down and we were more present, would that bring us balance and joy?

Now I am not trying to suggest you don't have breaks from your kids, because we all know that too is central to a healthy relationship with them and yourself. We do mistake our bond to our children as an inextricable link too complex to be separate from. Yet every mother requires a balance of separate and together. And mamas need their downtime. Mamas need a break.

But if we had more breaks from all the other distractions in life, just maybe we wouldn't need as many breaks from our kids.

I often hear mothers talk about how stressful being a mother is, and it is, but life too is stressful and so often we can miss these beautiful moments with our kids by getting caught up in all the things that have to be done or the worries and anticipation we have racing through our heads. We have to get the washing done, have to clean that floor for the second time this morning, have to buy food, have to make baby food, have to help with homework, have to exercise, have to pay the bills, have to get work done by deadline, have to have sex tonight, have to ring my mother, have to, have to, have to.

The "have tos" are stressful and they load our plates and our kids only need to tap our plate for us to lose it all.

There are always so many "have tos", too many obligations, too many things. There is never enough white space, freedom and just being with those we love.

In his book *The Power of Now*, Eckhart Tolle says 'As soon as you honour the present moment, all unhappiness and struggle dissolve, and life begins to flow with joy and ease.'

How do we find presence? I think we start by asking ourselves what is most important. Tick off the essentials: money to pay for food and our home and transport. Next think about what really matters. Your kids are growing up faster by the minute, how they are right now is the littlest they are going to be ever again. Their voices change, their small clothes become bigger, that glisten in their eye for Mummy changes. They will find themselves and one day once you have done your job so well, they won't need you as much (insert shattered mama hearts across the globe)

Doesn't this matter more than anything else? Why do we escape this when we should be escaping all the things that take us away from those we love?

Your dreams

Infuse your life with action. Don't wait for it to happen. Make it happen. Make your own future. Make your own hope. Make your own love. And whatever your beliefs, honour your creator, not by passively waiting for grace to come down from upon high, but by doing what you can to make grace happen... yourself, right now, right down here on Earth.

— BRADLEY WHITFORD

Back when we were little, we dreamed of all the possibilities that awaited us in our lives. Our dreams may have seemed somewhat idealistic then. We wanted to reach for the highest star in the sky and wouldn't listen to the naysayers who told us we will never reach it.

No matter how wild, challenging or unachievable our dream may have been, we didn't care. It was ours after all, and isn't that what a dream is for? It's ours to own, ours to work towards until it becomes a reality.

Generally, as kids, we stop at nothing to make our dreams come true, but as adults, we become more "realistic" and start placing limitations and restrictions on what we can and can't have, crossing dreams off our lists as if they were merely a vanishing twinkle in the eye of our younger selves.

I'm a big dreamer, never short of my next inspiring idea or adventure - I definitely don't lack the inspiration. I'll reach for the stars, yet in the past I've lacked action and manifestation.

I could dream the rest of my life away, no dramas, but up to this point, not all of my dreams have eventuated. The creation is not my problem, it is working against my self-limiting beliefs that is my final barrier to success.

I have often put my dreams in that "too hard" or "who am I to do that?" basket and then felt disappointment with myself.

Don't I owe so much more to myself than to give up on my dreams so easily? But as I am here writing this, I remind myself that despite all the moments in life when I have let my dreams go, right now I am making a new, awesome and inspiring dream happen, which is to write this book.

Turns out I *can* make things happen and I do have it within myself to believe that I am worthy of any dream I choose.

And really, who are we without our dreams? By not acknowledging them and not making them a reality, we ultimately are denying a core part of our soul. We are basically telling ourselves that our dreams (and therefore we) aren't worthy, and so we let go of them.

We all have these passions and desires to create and live a life that feels fulfilling to our hearts. Making this all happen means we need to put into practise all the self-love lessons and practices we have been working on.

You have a newfound appreciation for the magnificent woman you are and all you represent. Self-love has become an integral part of your life, you stand up for what you believe in, you worry less about others' opinions, you are embracing your mama bod in the way it deserves to be, and you are actively practising acceptance and forgiveness.

In your own quiet way, you are living with grace each and every day, and you have everything you could possibly need to start living your dreams. Once the inner you is flourishing you have all the tools you need to make your external world flourish too.

Achieving your own dreams is not selfish. Sacrificing ourselves and our dreams in an effort to be a "good mother" is doing no one any favours. Acknowledging that you need more for yourself may have been what lead you to this book in the first place.

You, just as much as everyone else, deserve the time and opportunity to achieve your innermost desires. I'm talking about the biggest, no-limitations, no-excuses, heart-pumping, soul-quenching, body-tingling, wildest hopes and dreams you can come up with. Don't let your ego creep in and start telling you it's selfish, or you're too old to make it happen, or it's not financially possible, or who do you think you are to do something like that anyway?

I release all fear that is holding me back.
It is my birthright to have dreams.
I will achieve all my heart desires.

When was the last time you let your mind run free with your dreams and desires without immediately placing a restriction on them? When did you truly believe you can create the life you want without any resistance?

We love to make excuses, sometimes before we even start. But your dreams are way fiercer than your excuses. You just need to believe that you too are worthy.

Minus the excuses, what do you want in this life? I'm not going to place a lid on your dream jar and you shouldn't either. Your dreams can be big or small, wild or reasonable. Whatever they may be, let yourself imagine them.

I encourage you to start a fresh page in your journal for this exercise and to close your eyes, breathe, visualize and feel your dreams and just write.

Follow the feeling of the dream right through your body until it comes out of the pen and onto the paper. Play music if you like or sit in silence. Do whatever you think will bring out your inner dream weaver.

- What are your dreams?
- What magic lies within you that you need to share?
- What does your soul crave when it speaks to you in the silence?
- What ignites the passion and sense of purpose in you?
- What must you see, do and feel in this lifetime to consider it whole?

Take all of the inspiration from these questions and use them as the foundation for a dream board. For those of you who are unfamiliar with the concept of a dream board, it is a visualisation tool that helps us remember and connect with what we want in our lives. It works on the spiritual laws of attraction and abundance.

Include words, feelings, pictures – anything that moves you or inspires your dreams. Include happy pictures of your family and add those cute and indistinguishable *It's a fire truck, Mummy!* paintings from the kids.

To give you an idea of where to go with this, my dream board is a magnetic board that I have stuck above my desk. On it are inspirational quotes, tarot cards that I alternate, photos of my family, and images of places I would love to see. There are also pictures of a guitar and a surfboard to encourage my dream to learn.

Every time I look at it, I am reminded of what I am already eternally grateful to have in my life, as well as what I am aspiring to bring into it.

The second equally important part of this process is taking that leap of faith. We can feel all we want into our dreams, but if we never take appropriate action, then how can we expect them to materialise into anything?

If it's a holiday you're dreaming of, then open a savings account and start depositing money into it each week, even if it is only a couple of dollars. If it's learning an instrument, then book in for a lesson or find a YouTube clip to get you started. If it's a new career you want, do some research or go to college open days.

Any step you take, no matter how small, brings your dream closer to reality. It will likely take lots of small steps, but just start walking.

What promise can you make to yourself that brings you one step closer to your dreams?

Returning to grace

Motherhood in all its beautiful madness is an experience to behold. You can't explain it until you're in it… and even then, the words fall short. Some days it is beautiful, other days you will go mad. How do we return to grace when we feel disconnected from ourselves or on those days when it all seems to be falling apart?

Grace is there for us in every moment. Remember it is about learning to come home, you now know what home feels like and how to welcome grace into your life.

Living the practice of conscious motherhood every day is just that, a practice. There will be hiccups and challenges because life is only doing its best when it's forcing us to grow and adapt but you've been through enough to know you will get through this. You know enough to be able to witness those self-limiting beliefs and societal expectations before they overwhelm you.

Breathe. Take a deep breath in and let it out slowly. Don't rush the breath. Feel it. Let it go through you, relax you and re-centre you.

Don't underestimate the life force that is our breath, it can have incredible effects on our nervous system, but you have to be willing to surrender and let your breath guide you.

You can calm your anxiety, clear your mind and get clarity on what's next when you slow down through your breath.

Simplify. How can I remove my expectations, fear and self-limiting beliefs and make this simpler? We attach our feelings into experiences and get wound up in our emotions and worrying about potential outcomes but there may be a simpler solution.

If there is no solution and it is out of your control, simplify how you feel about it. *How can this be less complicated for me?*

Go inwards. Once you are calm, ask your inner wisdom what you need.

Our minds are busy and will create more confusion than we need. Your wisdom is already within you, the next step, the advice, your answers are within. That knowledge gives you peace and power.

First check in with yourself if you have a solution or some comfort before you attempt to seek that externally. *What do I/we need right now, in this moment? What will best serve all involved?*

Embrace. If it's just one of those days and no amount of breathing, calmness or lateral thinking will work, then embrace the madness. Days like these come out of nowhere and are gone just as quickly. You are not failing as a mother or a human being if you have a day of being angry and pissed off about sibling fighting and toddler meltdowns.

This is mum life. Go easy on yourself and know that it's okay to have bad days. There is always another tomorrow.

I release all that no longer serves me.
I accept what is.
I invite grace into my life now.

Love is all you need

Remember that wherever your heart is,
there you will find your treasure.
— PAULO COELHO

In that moment our first child, Jacob, was born I have two distinct memories, the first being the sound of Jacob's cry, which was the most beautiful sound I had ever heard. The second memory was the sound of Spooner's voice when he said "There he is."

I'd never heard his voice sound like that before. A joy and love that was boundless was expressed all in those three words.

The sound of Jacob's cry and Spooner's voice will be etched in time forever.

Spooner spoke in the same tone at the birth of every child… and even at the ultrasound when we found out Daddy would finally get his little girl.

Becoming a mother cracked my heart open in a way I never imagined possible. From the first moment I saw the beautiful faces of my children to this very day when I see them with beaming smiles or sleeping soundly in their beds, the same unconditional, unbreakable love floods through me.

A parent's love knows no bounds; it is all-encompassing, and I will be forever grateful that I've been blessed to experience it.

I would do anything for my family of five. *Anything.* My love for them is what drove me to change, to rediscover myself and be present as

I know they deserve me to be.

We are all so fortunate to have the love of family in our lives. When we take away all the stress, material stuff and everything we think we need to make our lives better, in the end, all we really need is love. This love is what ultimately makes us want to be the best version of ourselves we can be.

To say that being a parent is a tough job falls well short of the reality, and saying that it's a life you can never prepare for also doesn't quite cover it.

In your time as a mum, whether it's been days, weeks or years, you will have found your friendships have been tested and maybe broken and your relationship with your partner has been subjected to intense stress. You may have been forced to deal with mental or physical disease. Your child or children may have fallen ill or been born with a medical condition.

As a mother, you will have been required, day after day after day, to face challenges, doubts, fears, criticisms, uncertainty, exhaustion, frustration, anger and sadness, alongside the awe, wonder, delight, surprise, joy and simple contentment. Your moods may swing from happy one day to shattered the next. You may be fighting until you are blue in the face or you could be living life like you're on cloud nine.

Whatever the case at any given time, we must constantly remind ourselves that the bad days will be followed by better ones.

Life will always be unpredictable when you're a parent (and just in general too!) and the only cure for the hard times is to dig deep with those we love. And we need to love ourselves with so much fierce abandon that we never feel deprived again.

Our self-love is the catalyst for all love, love yourself and you can in turn love all others with full acceptance and from a full heart.

The best way – and perhaps the only true way – to get through this beautiful madness is to just keep coming back to love.

Every chance you get, choose love over fear. Hold close and tight to those you love. Trust me when I tell you this is the most powerful and long-lasting therapy that you will ever find. Sometimes love really is all you need.

Continue to make the decision each time to choose love. When it is hard, love yourself. When you want to escape, love yourself. When you don't know the next step, choose a loving response.

We can't change the beautiful madness of motherhood, but we can learn to find love in every situation.

You deserve your own love and compassion, and it alone will be what gets you through the hardest of times. Love from someone else is not there when you are crying on the bathroom floor, you have to be comfortable with your own vulnerability and assured in your own strength. Your love for yourself has to be stronger than those moments to pull you out of it.

And it will be. You know your worth. You know you deserve to be loved. You know you are a wonderful mother and woman.

Remember this, Beautiful

We are almost at the end of our journey together, Beautiful. I'm so glad you have been with me on this mostly-beautiful and sometimes-mad path.

Along the way, you have delved into your soul and understood yourself in a whole new way. You listened to the calling of your inner power and honoured yourself. You reconnected with dreams and have fallen back in love with the magnificent woman that you are. You understand that the role of being a mother comes with unspoken and systemic expectations that we have all adopted but which do not serve us any longer.

You know that in order to thrive you need to do more than just survive. You know that being a "good mother" is inherently within you and that no one outside of you can judge that.

But your journey does not end here. It goes on and so do you.

On the good days and especially on the bad days, you will be called upon constantly to remember all the truths you know.

- Be kind to yourself.
- Always practise forgiveness.
- There is no space and no need for guilt in your life.
- You are not alone in these feelings.
- Caring for yourself is imperative to be able to care for others.
- There is no such thing as failure.
- Just because you think something doesn't make it true.

- You are undoing lifetimes of systemic structure so that you can thrive (go you!).
- Every mother has the same feelings, fears and doubts as you do – and it's all normal.
- You are entitled to parent in the best way you know how, even when others question you.
- You cannot make mistakes in your children's eyes, because they will always love you unconditionally.
- You are loved and appreciated by those around you even if you don't always see or hear it.
- Being honest about your struggles is a sign of strength, not weakness.
- You have the ability to change the direction of your life.
- Chasing your dreams and making changes in your life is not selfish.
- Believe that you are worthy.
- Don't compromise on what you need or who you are to make others feel comfortable.
- You deserve your own respect and love.
- Love will overcome everything.

Conclusion

When I think about now compared to then, about me compared to her, it's like opposite realities in the same world. She and I are one in the same yet I have never felt more myself than I do right now. Where I am now and who I am proud to be today was always within my reach, yet I spent so long being disconnected from that. I see the wisdom in my lessons, the divine and perfect timing of how it had to play out. When I am kind to myself, I can admit that I am proud of how far I have come. Only I know the demons I was battling, and only I know the crushing limitations I imposed on my own existence. So, with kindness in my heart, I can truthfully say I've done a pretty good job of finding myself amid all that mess. If one day my children ask me about my book, I'll tell them I wrote it not just for the mamas, but for their children and loved ones as well. I'll tell them I wrote it in the hope that no mother would ever question her value, be fearful or alone in her world, or feel as though she has lost touch with herself. I hope one day that my children too will read it and appreciate the importance of this journey of parenting. I will be proud to tell them their mummy was honest, kind and even forgiving at a time when those simple things seemed so hard. I can at last give a name to what it is I've been chasing this whole time. Grace. It sums up everything I've been dreaming of and the life I hoped I could achieve for myself and our family. It's

*taken me a while to find it, but one thing I know for sure is that
once you've touched grace, it's impossible to forget that feeling.*

So here we are, beautiful Mama, at the end of the journey back to yourself. I hope you will feel great pride and satisfaction in every step you have taken along the way.

It takes courage to go on a journey of self-discovery and to question all that binds you in order to be truly free. You accepted the invitation to heal within and reconnect with your truest self. You committed to changing your perspective from the old stories we have been told, to the new version of conscious motherhood that welcomes truth and acceptance as pillars of parenting. I know from my own experience that your life won't ever be quite the same again. How could it be when you have literally reshaped and freed yourself to become the truest, most magnificent version of you?

For me, this journey of self-discovery and reconnection has been life-changing.

I started out, perhaps like you did, feeling depressed, anxious, uncertain, fearful and lost. Every musing and piece of advice I have offered to you in this book is one I learned and embraced myself. This whole journey has left me enlightened, confident, accepting, and filled with a deep knowing that everything will always be okay in the end.

Your journey will have been different to mine, but I trust that as you peruse these final pages you really can feel a shift in your presence from the woman who began reading this book to the one who reads it now.

We started out on our path together by getting in touch with our fears, what we felt was holding us back and what we hoped for our future. We realised that all of us mums are on this journey together, fumbling our way through mum life together. We released our attachment to unhelpful emotions like guilt, comparison and shame and in so doing, we created space for acknowledgement, acceptance and forgiveness.

We now understand that we mothers are a product of society and the stories that have been created around the mother archetype. We discovered that so much of our strain has come from trying to fit into that box, yet we know within ourselves that balance, freedom and happiness comes from not fitting in at all.

We learnt that it is imperative to practise self-love and take care of our mind, body and spirit in order to be able to love and care for those around us. We reconnected with the woman we thought we had lost and reinvented her for her new life as a mother. We embraced our miracle-making bodies and learnt about the true beauty we have on the inside and the outside.

We understand now the importance of honesty, connection and support, and how all of this plays an integral role in helping us cope with the challenges of being a mother.

We know for certain that mental illness should never be a cause of shame for ourselves or anyone else.

We learned that we can tune into our own inner wisdom to gently bring ourselves back to grace.

My wish is that this book has empowered you as much as it has empowered me, not only when I worked through these experiences myself, but also as I sat here typing away and pouring my soul into it. From the moment I decided to make this a reality, my passion to serve you has been unrelenting.

Every woman I spoke to about her experience of mothering inspired me to keep going and convinced me that this book needed to be written; that my story and the story of all of us mums needs to be told. The real and unedited version of motherhood. The one that challenges the pretty and acceptable archetype of conformed motherhood. The *real* version that refuses to let any mother be being put in any kind of box.

Because talking about the expectations we place on mothers is the first step in breaking our chains. Our stories need to be heard, they need to be honoured and something needs to change.

By picking up this book, you have shared in these stories and have shifted the energy in your life. That shift may have inspired another mama to get on board with some vital self-love, or it could mean that your relationships have become stronger and more honest. Your approach to parenting, and indeed your view of yourself, have no doubt taken on a new conscious perspective now that you are living as your authentic self.

I want to thank you for having the courage to welcome these changes into your life, but also acknowledge that in doing so, you have made it possible for other mums and mums-to-be to do the same.

As a collective, we mothers have the potential to influence how society perceives us. Within each of us is a stunning combination of power and unconditional love, and we are being called to use it.

Together we can create a conscious shift in the world around us by crusading for perhaps the most crucial cause of all – one of love and acceptance. All of us living in a world where we are free from self-judgement, free from guilt, free from believing sacrifice is the only way to be, and free from the pressures of being perfect.

Through our choices and actions, we can let other mums know they are supported, heard, appreciated and loved and that the work they do will never go unnoticed again.

Every time one of us changes a false story or chooses love over fear, we are showing that it is possible to keep our balance and stay true to ourselves amid the beautiful madness of parenting. What's more, we are inviting our children to do the same for themselves and one day for their own children too.

Conscious motherhood is simply looking through a different lens. It is changing our perspective internally and externally about motherhood, what it should look like and what is acceptable. Conscious motherhood is like the warmest embrace that reminds you, you are divinely perfect and everything will be okay.

Although our time together is coming to an end, I know that you will continue to learn, grow and change on your journey as a woman and as a mother.

Your foundations moving forward are self-compassion, forgiveness and acceptance. Remind yourself that you would never be given any challenge you can't handle. I know you can do this, and you do too. Forgive and let go when you feel that all else is failing. Make a promise that you will love yourself so deeply, just as you are

This role we undertake as mums is challenging yet rewarding, exhausting yet fruitful, crazy yet divine. To survive it, and better still thrive in it, we must all make a lifelong commitment to be kind to ourselves, always know our own worth, and lovingly invite grace into our everyday lives.

Here, at the end of this book, I want to extend a never-ending gratitude and appreciation to you for having faith in the words I have offered you and for accepting me and my journey into your life. Thank you for starting your own journey with me.

There's one final point I want you to keep in mind before I say goodbye, and it is this:

YOU ARE DOING IT!

In this very moment and in all the moments since you became a mother, you have been doing it. Doing a great job, being an unwavering pillar of support, loving your children unconditionally, always looking out for their best interests, and taking care of them in the way that only their mother knows how.

You do your very best even when you don't have anything left, you always make sure everyone knows they are important... and now you can do all of this from a place of self-love and appreciation. *You are doing it, Mama.*

Your kids need you to be your best you. However old they are and whatever it is they need; *you* are important to them. No one could ever replace their mummy, and they love you just as you are.

Trust in that love. Let it hold you when you are in doubt. Let it fill every fibre of your being.

The love between a parent and child is extraordinary, everlasting and energetic. It will naturally ebb and flow, and at times you may feel stronger while at others you could feel divided. Sometimes the love you have for your children may even seem like it is too much for you to bear and the love they give you in return is almost overwhelming.

Never doubt, that this bond between you can save you both. It can set you free from heartache, show you the world with new eyes and remind you why you started searching for grace in the first place. They will bring you back home to yourself.

Despite all the madness of caring for our children and all life has sent our way, I am pleased to say that moments of grace have become easier for me to find these days.

I never once thought I would get here. But I did. Maybe my soul was calling to me for a long time to break down the walls and find what motherhood is truly meant to be. Maybe my soul was yearning to slow down, be content and remember what truly matters.

Maybe this journey was exactly what I had been waiting my whole life for... perhaps there are no maybes about it. I know that when I choose love over fear, miracles can and do happen.

One thing is for certain, I am deeply thankful for my realisation that this beautifully mad world and everything in it is exactly as it should be. I acknowledge this, I accept it and I appreciate it.

And that, Beautiful, is living with grace.

A note from Cathy

The stuff every mama needs to hear:

- You are doing the very best job the way you know how – and that is enough.
- Being a mother is the hardest role you will ever fulfil. Don't sell yourself short on what it takes to do what you are doing.
- Your children are blessed to have you as their mummy.
- Remember to nourish your own body and soul as well as those around you. A tired, resentful and overworked mama is no good to anybody.
- It's normal to feel guilty about some of your parenting decisions. Just don't hold onto that guilt. Accept the feelings and move on.
- Own your decisions. They are your children and your family, and it's your life. Don't let other people's opinions dictate how you should be living it.
- Don't judge yourself for your decisions, no matter what the circumstances are. You made the best decision with the tools available to you at the time.
- Making mistakes is part of the journey, and you are learning along the way. No mama before you got it right every time, and I doubt you will be the first to do so.
- Let go of the fear of not being good enough. It will ruin your chance at the life you deserve. You are good enough right now, exactly as you are.

- Holding onto resentment does more harm than good. Learn to forgive and let go wherever possible.

- Remember that our kids don't set out to drive us nuts, they are just experiencing this world and their emotions in their own way. They aren't out to get you, so don't take their crap personally.

- Your body is more beautiful now than it ever was before.

- Please ask for help. No one is handing out medals for the most resilient mum. If and when you're overwhelmed, forget fear and shame and just reach out to someone.

- Don't ever be ashamed of mental illness. It is more common than you realise and is a sign of the broken stories of motherhood, not a reflection on you.

- You prove each and every day how resilient and strong you are. Don't ever doubt the spirit within you.

- Be honest with those around you about how wild and full on your world can be. Truth will set you – and the rest of us mamas – free!

- Sleep whenever you can. For a deprived mama, sleep should be a priority over any household chore.

- Stay connected with your people. Whether it's your girlfriends, sister or mothers' group, stay in touch with whoever your fellow goddesses are. They will remind you of who you are.
  and help keep your head in check whenever you start veering sideways.

- No amount of spilt milk, smashed food, broken ornaments or poo-soaked car seats is ever worth the stress we place on it. Most of the time you can fix the situation, so breathe and let the stress go.

- Love your partner like you used to before you had kids. Be spontaneous, caring and sexy. Nourish your love, and together you will get through the biggest of storms.
- Accept that having children puts a tonne of strain on your relationships. Don't stay angry at your partner, they are probably stressed and overwhelmed too. Remember you're both doing the best you can.
- Don't judge other mums, ever. You can't know what is going on behind closed doors or in her heart and mind. It's never your place to judge.
- Show compassion and understanding to other mums. Even if you haven't experienced the rawness of particular parenting emotions, just show compassion. We deal with some heavy stuff as mamas, and knowing that those around us understand what we're going through even if they haven't been there themselves does make it a little bit easier.
- It's normal to feel on some days like you don't want to be a mother.
- It's normal to feel like maybe this gig isn't exactly what you thought you signed up for.
- You are not alone. If you are feeling it, then I can guarantee another mama out there has felt it too.
- Whether it's bottle or breast, as long as mum and baby are healthy and happy, it's best!
- Whether you stay at home or go to work, you are a champion mother.
- There is no medal for being it all and having it all. Drop the expectation and pressure, live your life how you want to live it, and forget trying to fit into the mould of being "perfect".

- Don't let social media bring doubt into your life. This is all curated and you can only see what they want you to see. Take it all with a grain of salt.
- Never underestimate the power of a guilt-free indulgence in chocolate (or wine, tea or other delight).
- Remember to have fun. A mum's life can get heavy sometimes, so try to lighten it up whenever you can.
- Dance when the chance arises. Every time.
- You deserve love. Tell yourself this and don't wait to hear it from someone else.
- Some days there will be no solution for your dramas. Just ride the storm and know that these moments will pass as quickly as they arrived.
- Everyone will always have advice for you, but you don't have to feel pressured to take them up on it.
- Take deep breaths when it gets too much.
- Remember that we are all in this together.
- You are doing a great job, Mama!

Resources

Scan the QR code below to access your free meditations,
EFT tapping training, visualisations and more.

Support:

Lifeline: 13 11 14

Panda Australia (PeriNatal Anxiety and Depression Australia):
1300 726 306

1800RESPECT: 1800 737 732

Beyond Blue: 1300 224 636

Gidget Foundation: 1300 851 758

SANDS (Miscarriage, Stillbirth and Newborn death support):
1300 308 307

Pregnancy Birth and Baby helpline: 1800 882 436

Acknowledgements

Spooner, you have always been my greatest mirror. You reflect back to me all the things about myself that I am unable to see and remind me I am always deserving of love. You amaze me with your capacity to be an incredible husband and father, we are all so thankful to have you. Thank you for holding me up when I couldn't myself and for reminding that true love will bend and stretch not because it can, but because it wants to. I love you darling.

Our beautiful children; Jacob, Harry and Ruby, thank you for always reminding me why life is so special and why it should always be respected and embraced with all my being. Without knowing it, your presence and unconditional love got me through the hardest of times. Thank you for choosing me to be your Mummy, you're my life and I love you endlessly.

Mum and Dad, thank you for believing in me and supporting me with all you had. Becoming a parent now I realise the honour that this responsibility entails and respect you so much for raising me to be someone who wants to help others. Mum, I miss you everyday but I know you have been watching over my shoulder with loving support as I've typed every word in this book.

My friends and family, they say raising a family takes a village, in becoming a mother I could not have done it without you. Thank you for being there even when you weren't sure how, for listening without judgement, for making me laugh and reminding me of all the goodness in me and all around me.

Natasha and the kind press team, I will be forever thankful for you believing in this book and valuing this dream as much as I did. Your capacity to honour the process, creativity and natural evolution of this book is testament to your talent and compassion as an editor. Thank you to the team for piecing this altogether, for bringing ideas and musings of love into one whole story that looks and sounds like the dream I envisioned. Thank you to Sian Yewdell for your publicity magic getting this book into the hands of all mamas who need it.

Charise, Fiona, Nicole and Phillippa, over the years you have all given me professional care in some of my most challenging moments, care that felt so much more to me than you just doing your job. Thank you for listening with all you heart, offering advice and making me feel like I would never be alone.

To everyone who helped me on my personal journey, my soul sisters who no matter how much time we are apart, show the fiercest and loving support of any venture we all undertake. Shunanda Scott for waking up, witnessing and honoring the spirit in me and helping me embody the truest expression of myself. Yvette Luciano for reminding me why our dreams and love are so important and how to share it with passion and authenticity. Tara Bliss for igniting my writing fire all those years ago and embodying your truth so we all feel inspired to do the same.

To all the mamas, your honesty, empathy, willingness to listen and share has helped remind me that I am not alone. Every interaction with friends, clients or acquaintances has reminded me why sharing my story, our stories, is important and imperative if there is to be change now and in the future.

About the author

Cathy Spooner

Cathy Spooner is a mother to three children, Life Coach and mum evolution crusader. She is the Creatrix of Woman Rising, an online course to help awaken the woman alongside the mother.

Her personal journey with postnatal depression, anxiety and children with additional needs inspired her to search within to find herself and to feel aligned in her life as a woman and mother.

Cathy helps empower women to release stress, expectation and overwhelm and reconnect with their truest self amid the beautiful madness of motherhood. She believes a conscious approach to motherhood that is focused on acceptance, self compassion and understanding will help to rewrite our perspective on motherhood.

Facebook /cathyspoonerauthor | Instagram @cathyspooner_author
www.cathyspooner.com.au